James W. Armstrong II

Sheila Parke

Emilio DeFraga

Ross Haray

UNDOCUMENTED

GREAT LAKES POETS LAUREATE ON SOCIAL JUSTICE

MENTED

Edited by Ron Riekki and Andrea Scarpino

Michigan State University Press | *East Lansing*

Louise Bogan's "Resolve" appeared in the August 1922 issue of
Poetry: A Magazine of Verse. Public domain.

"Lady Freedom Among Us," "Freedom Ride," and "Rosa" from *On the Bus with
Rosa Parks: Poems*, W.W. Norton & Company, New York, NY. © 1999 by Rita Dove.
Reprinted by permission of the author.

"Trayvon, Redux" was first published online by *The Root.* © 2013 by Rita Dove.
Reprinted by permission of the author.

"Ten Ways to Fight Hate: A Community Response Guide" excerpts are reprinted with
permission of Teaching Tolerance, a project of the Southern Poverty Law Center.

All other poems were previously unpublished and appear by permission
of the respective authors.

♾ The paper used in this publication meets the minimum requirements
of ANSI/NISO Z39.48-1992 (R 1997) (Permanence of Paper).

Michigan State University Press
East Lansing, Michigan 48823-5245

Printed and bound in the United States of America.

28 27 26 25 24 23 22 21 20 19   1 2 3 4 5 6 7 8 9 10

LIBRARY OF CONGRESS CATALOGING-IN-PUBLICATION DATA
Names: Riekki, R. A., editor. | Scarpino, Andrea, editor.
Title: Undocumented : Great Lakes poets laureate on social justice
/ edited by Ron Riekki and Andrea Scarpino.
Description: East Lansing : Michigan State University Press, [2019]
Identifiers: LCCN 2018011621 | ISBN 9781611863086 (pbk. : alk. paper)
| ISBN 9781609175870 (pdf) | ISBN 9781628953510 (epub) | ISBN 9781628963519 (kindle)
Subjects: LCSH: American poetry—Michigan. | Social justice—Poetry.
| Poets laureate—Michigan. | Michigan—Literary collections.
Classification: LCC PS571.M5 U53 2019 | DDC 811.008/09774—dc23
LC record available at https://lccn.loc.gov/2018011621

Book design by Charlie Sharp, Sharp Designs, East Lansing, MI
Cover design by Cover design by Erin Kirk New
Cover artwork is *8 Swords* © 2017 and is used courtesy of the artist,
Wendy Vardaman, with permission. All rights reserved.

Michigan State University Press is a member of the Green Press Initiative and is committed to developing
and encouraging ecologically responsible publishing practices. For more information about the Green
Press Initiative and the use of recycled paper in book publishing, please visit *www.greenpressinitiative.org.*

Visit Michigan State University Press at *www.msupress.org*

Contents

Act

"In the face of hate, silence is deadly. Apathy will be interpreted as acceptance—
by the perpetrators, the public, and—worse—the victims. If left unchallenged,
hate persists and grows."

Unite

"Call a friend or coworker. Organize allies from churches, schools, clubs, and other civic groups. Create a diverse coalition. Include children, police, and the media. Gather ideas from everyone, and get everyone involved."

Support Victims

"Let victims know you care. Support them with comfort and protection."

Do Your Homework

"An informed campaign improves its effectiveness."

Create an Alternative

"Every act of hatred should be met with an act of love and unity . . . Hold a unity rally or parade to draw media attention away from hate."

Speak Up

"Hate must be exposed and denounced . . . An informed and unified community is the best defense against hate."

Lobby Leaders

"Elected officials and other community leaders can be important allies [in the fight against hate]."

Look Long Range

"Expand your community's comfort zones so you can learn and live together."

Teach Tolerance

"Bias is learned early, often at home. Schools can offer lessons in tolerance and
acceptance. Host a diversity and inclusion day on campus. Reach out to young
people who may be susceptible to hate group propaganda and prejudice."

Dig Deeper

"Tolerance, fundamentally, is a personal decision. It comes from an attitude that is learnable and embraceable: a belief that every voice matters, that all people are valuable, that no one is 'less than' . . . Look inside yourself for prejudices and stereotypes. Build your own cultural competency, then keep working to expose discrimination wherever it happens—in housing, employment, education, and more."

What Can You Do?

"Pick up the phone. Call friends and colleagues. Host a neighborhood or community meeting. Speak up in church. Suggest some action. Sign a petition. Attend a vigil. Lead a prayer. Report acts of hate-fueled vandalism, as a neighborhood or a community. Use whatever skills and means you have. Offer your print shop to make fliers. Share your musical talents at a rally. Give your employees the afternoon off to attend. Be creative. Take action. Do your part to fight hate."

Lisa Russ Spaar

Foreword

W. H. Auden is often evoked when the relevance of poetry to polis comes up. "Poetry," Auden professes in his "In Memory of W.B. Yeats," "makes nothing happen." Another poet, the New Jersey physician William Carlos Williams, had his own spin on the relationship of poetry to the world: "It is difficult," he wrote in "Asphodel, That Greeny Flower," "to get the news from poems / yet men die miserably every day / for lack / of what is found there."

Does poetry matter when it comes to changing humanity for the better? Are poets, as Percy Bysshe Shelley proclaimed, "the unacknowledged legislators of the world?" At a time when our elected officials seem incapable of solving global and local crises, and journalism often seems less and less equal to the task of presenting the news factually and clearly, is there something inimitable that poetry—particularly the poems of those poets we honor with the title "Poet Laureate" as representatives of our collective city, state, and national identities—can offer?

This anthology of poems, nearly all of them new and previously unpublished, and dealing with issues of social justice, written by current and former city, state, and Canadian Parliamentary and U.S. Poets Laureate with ties to the Great Lakes region, suggests that what Ezra Pound said about literature—that it is "news that stays news"—is true. The Great Lakes region is a large, rich, and varied place that is written into place by many of its Laureates, but the myriad subjects broached by these honored poets—what they say *about* and *from* this particular place—are relevant to citizens everywhere. Issues of ecology, race, violence, family, inequity, work, power, usurpation, language, education, religion, animal rights, gender dynamics, and more illuminate each other with the turn of every page. "Touch the universe anywhere," writes A. R. Ammons, "and you touch it everywhere." Or, as Rita Dove, former Poet Laureate of the United States, writes in "Lady Freedom Among Us,"

> *don't think you can ever forget her*
> *don't even try*
> *she's not going to budge*
>
> *no choice but to grant her space*
> *crown her with sky*
> *for she is one of the many*
> *and she is each of us*

Editors' Notes

The chapter headings are from the SPLC's "Ten Ways to Fight Hate: A Community Response Guide," reprinted courtesy of the Southern Poverty Law Center.

With the exception of poems by Louise Bogan and Rita Dove, all of the poems in this anthology have never been published before. All of the poetry in this collection is written by current or previous city, county, state, or U.S. Poets Laureate, or Canada Parliamentary Poets Laureate.

Who We Are, What Is Ours: An Introduction

As we all do, we attempt to advance our individual agendas through whatever means appropriate—this time through our written works. In the case of this anthology, Poets Laureate have the rare opportunity, even obligation, to know their audiences, to appeal to their histories, to have a conversation of metaphoric language—good poets avoid fluff, the "have a nice day" poem, the work that is polite and precious. As I describe some of the purposes of this anthology of the works of Poets Laureate, this is only my opinion; see whether you agree.

This anthology gives you an opportunity to be engaged with the writer's history and immediate experience. We pull it into the whole of ourselves, to see if we can identify. Through a description of those aspects, we intend not only to inform readers, but to engage them with a sense of an agenda, a sense of urgency, a sense of priority. Not always, but I think it is important that we do so. Percy Bysshe Shelley says we are the legislators of the world, and I use that assignment to make and break man-made law, by practicing human law. I enjoy these poems of our Poets Laureate who address the significance of our contributions in this fashion.

Brace yourselves: Some call for radical change, and while poems are most effective when they describe and not prescribe, my particular bucky-horse is my truck with the use of Native American mascots and you better believe I'm about to not only describe the issue, but also demand prescribed behavior. My poem "Indian War" was presented to the Wisconsin legislative body; the entourage demanded the passage of a bill that described the cause and effect of the use of mascots and the effects on all children, largely hurtful. We issued a mandate to our teachers. The bill was passed without dissension. We ought never be marked by our indifference. We are complicit with the oppressor if we remain silent.

Silence is the voice of complicity, and I will have no part of that.

Poets Laureate might engage in a simple conversation; they may also be informational poets. Our histories as Poets Laureate become more significant to our audiences if we, at the very beginning, describe the function and responsibilities that belong to a Poet Laureate as I understand it. One taxpaying citizen said it like this: "What the devil is a Poet Laureate, and what am I paying for it?"

We define our roles in literary society, and almost always advocate for literacy, and as for our salary? My state no longer taps into any particular tax fund; any honorarium is funded by grants, departmental budgets, or fundraising. As a four-year Poet Laureate, I could not have it in any other way. It speaks to the monetary value of poetry, of which there is little. One poet remarks, "Poets are born, not paid," and that is the brutal truth of it.

The excellence of this anthology is in its sense of scope and the privilege to engage our audiences through the wisdom of the carefully written word. At its best, poetry is beautiful through its musical voice alone. Under the current administration, which has an agenda of its own, there is a leader who could give two flips about Poets Laureate, especially at his inauguration; that ought to be troublesome alone, especially when a world leader may have the comprehension of a fifth grader. Still, Poets Laureate are able to establish their credibility by being chosen a Poet Laureate. The selection committee must've thought we were up to the assignment, where it is impossible for the current administration to care less.

Post-election, there was a time where we felt powerless and discouraged as writers and as tax-paying citizens. My solution is to join the international tax resisters movement. I may end up in jail. Very well. There are things worth fighting for. In Latin America, my compadres have had pistols forced into their mouths by the security forces, their weapons their tongues. There are some things that call for civil disobedience. The Tibetans also feel there are some things worth dying for. Should it come to that, I can name a couple.

The focus, in my opinion, is to describe our shared experience; the ideal is to show we have alternatives, maybe even a radical route, away from the status quo. Because of the alternatives, many of us are not part of the status quo, and that's a damned shame. Why should we be a part of that?

Poet and Poet Laureate (York, Pennsylvania) Carla Christopher also must break man-made laws. In her poem "A System Cannot Fail," she states (and perhaps with a personal history): "If I don't break the law, / maybe they won't kill me . . . If I promise not to defend myself against their weapons, / maybe they won't kill me . . . If I don't breathe, / maybe they won't kill me." Our Latin American partners in crime do not comply with such a ridiculous flex of power on behalf of any corrupt state. Rob Hardy, Poet Laureate for Northfield, Minnesota, in his poem "My Mother's Pussy Hat" pays proper respect to the radical pussy movement,

> *my mother's pussy hat was one*
> *of millions, as if with enough pink yarn*
> *women could knit a whole nation back together.*

Another fave is M. L. Liebler's poem "American Psalm: Viola Liuzzo —American Hero," which speaks to the desire of many poets in other countries. Liebler is Poet Laureate for St. Clair Shores, Michigan.

> "I don't want to be your hero . . . I just want to fight like everyone else."
> —Joe Keefe, "Hero"

> *I come from a place*
> *Where unspoken heroes*
> *Are born to make a difference*
> *And are never heard from again.*

While I would love to carry on about this delightful, forceful, and necessary anthology, my page limit has been surpassed. America, this is our letter to the world. We are about the business of being a force, of being a part of the most important we might expect. It's time we had this talk.

For heaven's sake, I name each and every poem as my favorite, no kidding. You will have favorites too. To my friends as Poets Laureate, I am honored by your skill with the carefully spoken word; I pledge my support so desperately needed among working writers. As a poet of witness, and a poet of protest, I find our agendas quite compatible. This is who we are, this is what is ours. Carry on, mis amigos, as though your life depended upon it.

Andrea Scarpino Poet Laureate of the Upper Peninsula, Michigan

Prologue

When I moved to Michigan's Upper Peninsula in 2010, I knew very little about the Great Lakes other than they looked more like oceans as I flew over them on the way to Marquette. Soon, I learned about Lake Superior's red, orange, and yellow cliffs, its sandy beaches, its black rocks, its cold that took my breath away when I jumped into it, its hundreds of miles of trails through forests filled with deer and black bear, its snow and ice. I learned the Great Lakes contain one-fifth of Earth's surface freshwater, and that the region supports an estimated 6,000 species, some of them rare or endangered, like the piping plover found in Michigan, Wisconsin, and parts of Ontario.

I also learned that even its most pristine-appearing areas have been dramatically altered by humans. Hundreds of years of mining and manufacturing have contaminated the Great Lakes region with lead and PCBs among a long list of toxic substances, and companies up and down the lakes have used them as dumps for raw sewage and industrial waste. Poor air quality and smog abound. Dozens of radioactive hot spots in New York alone still await cleanup from Niagara Falls–area industries. Areas of gross contamination dot the landscape: By my count of the National Priority List, the Great Lakes region contains nearly 500 Superfund sites.

Since Ron first asked me to co-edit this anthology with him, I have conceived of our project as the best poets of our time—our poets laureate—writing about the most pressing issues of our time: topics like environmental degradation and climate change, race and racism, gender and sexism, the fight for the rights of indigenous peoples, police brutality, the politics and humanitarian issues surrounding immigration and refugees, our ongoing wars. There are so many issues demanding our attention that reading the news can feel overwhelming, destabilizing, paralyzing. And this is even more the case when our elected leaders don't seem to share our beliefs about these issues or our priorities in solving them. How do we advocate for the environmental integrity of the Great Lakes and our Earth (and thus, for the future of humanity) when the head of the Environmental Protection Agency doesn't believe in climate change? How do we discuss sexual violence when the President of the United States was caught on tape openly discussing assaulting women?

We turn to our poets.

We need our poets now more than ever to tackle these issues, to give us a sense of the scope of our disaster, and to imagine new solutions. We need our poets to remind us of the power of people working together, that our collective action can create big changes. We need our poets to remind us to continue fighting for equality. We need our poets to remind us of our shared humanity.

In the introduction to her seminal anthology *Against Forgetting: Twentieth-Century Poetry of Witness*, Carolyn Forché asks us to consider to whom the poet bears witness when she writes politically minded poetry. Forché writes, "In an age of atrocity, witness becomes an imperative and a problem: how does one bear witness to suffering and before what court of law?" When political institutions fail to protect the individual or actively cause the situation to which poetry must bear witness, identifying the audience for the poet's witnessing can be difficult. But in Forché's view, poetry of witness isn't necessarily intended to cause institutional or governmental change; it instead stands as stark reminder, as memory, as evidence of what occurred. Poetry stands *against forgetting* that something terrible is happening. In the words of Azade Seyhan, "Writing the terror painstakingly re-membered breaks the silences of history."

Take the poem "Trayvon, Redux" included here from former U.S. Poet Laureate Rita Dove, which begins with this epigraph from William Carlos Williams: "It is difficult / to get the news from poems / yet men die miserably every day / for lack / of what is found there." Dove's poem ends with the lines,

> *Here's a fine basket of riddles:*
> *If a mouth shoots off and no one's around*
> *to hear it, who can say which came first—*
> *push or shove, bang or whimper?*
> *Which is news fit to write home about?*

Here, Dove considers the problems of witnessing: To whom does one write the news of another Black man's violent death? Who is listening? But even as she asks these questions, she insists upon the urgency of witnessing, the urgency of recording these deaths and keeping the names of the dead in our minds, the urgency of understanding clearly the political and social situation in which we are living.

And our Great Lakes Poets Laureate are especially primed to witness. From the youth Poets Laureate of New York City, Chicago, and Philadelphia to the Poets Laureate across Ontario and Minnesota, they are incredibly diverse, they are engaged with their communities and the larger world around them, and they write what they know, whether the problems of inner city life, the problems of suburban sprawl, the problems of disappearing wilderness, or the problems of life on Reservations.

For example, in "History Lesson," Oscar Mireles describes the power of four women holding signs to protest the deportation of Mexicans from Minnesota in the 1920s. Although their actions aren't able to stop the deportations, they still stand waving their signs "as the last rain / fell into the sunset." They bear witness to atrocity, just as the poet bears witness to it in his poem. In "Red White and Blue Seuss," Zora Howard riffs on the classic children's book to bring to the forefront police brutality against people of color, what she calls "Black boy / Doctrine." Her poem reminds us to stay awake in the face of brutality, and that violence doesn't define us. In the last lines of the poem, Howard writes, "Light begets / Us fire won't / End us." And Joel Lipman's visual poem, "HOW MA / NY FLAGS / WERE TOO / MANY FLA / GS FOR / THE DEAD" asks us to consider patriotism, especially how we teach patriotism to children, and what it means to ask citizens to die for their country. These poems are very different in form, tone, and content; together, they demonstrate the breadth of contemporary poetry in the Great Lakes region, and the dedication of our Poets Laureate to tackle complicated and challenging issues.

One of our goals in this anthology was to be as inclusive as possible in accepting new work from local, state, and national Poets Laureate with ties to the Great Lakes region, including new work from former U.S. Poets Laureate and from Canada's current and former Parliamentary Poets Laureate. This means including work from people of different ethnicities, genders, cultural backgrounds, sexual orientations, religious beliefs, ages, and abilities who write in different forms, and tackle different subject matters. In other words, we wanted this anthology to be a book for the people, by the people, and thus, to include as vast a cross section of human experience as possible. Because our current issues are so pressing, so complex, so multifaceted, we felt we needed as many voices and experiences as possible to accurately represent them on the page.

It's interesting to note that some areas of the Great Lakes region have many more Poets Laureate than others. Pennsylvania, for example, seems to have a Poet Laureate for practically every county, while Indiana only has a few outside the official state position. Michigan hasn't had a state Poet Laureate since Edgar A. Guest ended his tenure in 1959, but Detroit, Lansing, Ann Arbor, Grand Rapids, St. Clair Shores, Three Oaks, and the Upper Peninsula have created their own positions. Some regions have chosen to separately honor Youth Poets Laureate. Some Poets Laureate have a one- or two-year term, while others serve for decades. And some regions have been choosing local Poets Laureate since the 1970s, while others have only recently begun a Poet Laureate program.

No matter their location or situation, the poets in *Undocumented* ground their work in our most pressing social issues. They ask us to challenge our current education system, our current prison system, our current health care system. They ask us to consider the harm being done to real-life bodies, female bodies and disabled bodies and brown bodies and poor bodies and bodies that don't live through the assaults they suffer. They ask us to consider the harm being done to our Earth. They challenge us to think in new ways, to imagine new alternatives to our current beliefs and social structures.

The poems in *Undocumented* remind us that our problems are human-caused and thus have human answers. They remind us that *we* are what's at stake, that our future on this planet depends on us finding solutions to our problems. They remind us to look deeply at one another, to listen deeply to one another, to pay attention, to remember. They ask us to take action. They prioritize our shared humanity. They bear witness. They stand against the silences of history.

REFERENCES

Forché, Carolyn, ed. *Against Forgetting: Twentieth-Century Poetry of Witness*. New York: W. W. Norton & Company, 1993.

Seyhan, Azade. "Enduring Grief: Autobiography as 'Poetry of Witness' in the Work of Assia Djebar and Nazim Hikmet." *Comparative Literature Studies* 40 (2003): 159–172.

Louise Bogan United States Poet Laureate (lived in New York)

Resolve

So that I shall no longer tarnish with my fingers
The bright steel of your power,
I shall be hardened against you,
A shield tightened upon its rim.

A stern oval to be pierced by no weapon,
Metal stretched and shaped against you.
For a long time I shall go
Spanned by the round of my strength.

Changeless, in spite of change,
My resolve undefeated;
Though now I see the evening moon, soon to wane,
Stand clearly and alone in the early dark,
Above the stirring spindles of the leaves.

Rita Dove United States Poet Laureate (born in Akron, Ohio)

Rosa

How she sat there,
the time right inside a place
so wrong it was ready.

That trim name with
its dream of a bench
to rest on. Her sensible coat.

Doing nothing was the doing:
the clean flame of her gaze
carved by a camera flash.

How she stood up
When they bent down to retrieve
her purse. That courtesy.

ACT

"In the face of hate, silence is deadly. Apathy will be interpreted as acceptance—by the perpetrators, the public, and—worse—the victims. If left unchallenged, hate persists and grows."

Rita Dove United States Poet Laureate (born in Akron, Ohio)

Trayvon, Redux

> It is difficult / to get the news from poems / yet men die miserably every day /
> for lack / of what is found there. / Hear me out / for I too am concerned / and
> every man / who wants to die at peace in his bed / besides.
>
> — William Carlos Williams, "Asphodel, that Greeny Flower"

Move along, you don't belong here.
This is what you're thinking. Thinking
drives you nuts these days, all that
talk about rights and law abidance when
you can't even walk your own neighborhood
in peace and quiet, *get your black ass gone.*
You're thinking again. Then what?
Matlock's on TV and here you are,
vigilant, weary, exposed to the elements
on a wet winter's evening in Florida
when all's not right but no one sees it.
Where are they—the law, the enforcers
blind as a bunch of lazy bats can be,
holsters dangling from coat hooks above their desks
as they jaw the news between donuts?

Hey! It tastes good, shoving your voice
down a throat thinking only of sweetness.
Go on, choke on that. Did you say something?
Are you thinking again? Stop!—and
get your ass gone, your blackness,
that casual little red riding hood
I'm just on my way home attitude

3

as if this street was his to walk on.
Do you hear me talking to you? Boy.
How dare he smile, jiggling his goodies
in that tiny shiny bag, his black paw crinkling it,
how dare he tinkle their laughter at you.

Here's a fine basket of riddles:
If a mouth shoots off and no one's around
to hear it, who can say which came first—
push or shove, bang or whimper?
Which is news fit to write home about?

Crystal Valentine New York City Youth Poet Laureate

I Do Not Trust People Who Hang American Flags on Their Front Porches

like predators displaying a gnawed carcass,
still wet and furnace enough to keep its bones warm
but not breathing, in front of their howling wasteland
with the carcass's mangled fur serving as the only welcome mat.

I know a man who carries a gun in his front pocket
just to remind me he can scatter my pulse across my front yard
without a newspaper making a sound.

The man, of course, is my president.
The gun, his cabin that he chauffeurs around
like a freshly polished ammunition belt.

Once he caught my eye through the television set,
held it for so long that my mother had to run
and get the Bible, lay hands on me,
whisper prayers to a God
who did not spare her father.

Now she doesn't ask why I don't watch Fox Five,
why I look away from the screen, cover my eyes
as if my ears can't see the bullets too.

I will only watch the news if God's mouth appears
in front of a blue charted screen in place of the anchorman,
apologizes as his tongue splits his lips into another eulogy:

5

And on Tuesday there is a 50 percent chance
of mothers wading across sidewalks once christened
by their daughters' double-dutch cord.
And on Wednesday bullets will hail from the sky
upon River Park Towers and we will only
cover the story about the mother who threw
her baby from the tower's gasping window
hoping the river's arms would baptize her child
before she is transferred, like so many other
wet and wailing bodies, to my front steps.
And Thursday will be the 3rd day in a row
that Jimmy does not rise from his casket
and the police will have to come stop his father
from clawing at the state-owned soil with his bare hands.
And on Friday—

When you are housed in a body as dark and shifting as mine
there will always be a casket overflowing with new names for rain.

Once, the American flag draped its cotton body
over my God's good sermon and my family
down in South Carolina went up in flames.
A whole generation on my mother's side contorted to ash
because their throats could not devour their own smoke.

My mother asked if I wanted to wear pigtails to the funeral,
like I did when I was a child.

That flag curves in the wind like a smile
right next to your front door.

Kimberly Blaeser Wisconsin Poet Laureate

Of the many ways to say: *Please Stand*

1. ∂, Partial Differential Equation

What we erase from polite conversation. Bodies on fire. The historic cleansing of the landscape, the sweep of humanity west, west, west. Environmental r ism.

All things being equal, things are never equal. Think of scope. Like the reach of the imperial. Or consider variables. Value. Or commodity. Ways of seeing. *Seven generations into the past; seven generations into the future.* Angles and perspectives. Convenience policy, a tally mark across generations. Uranium mining. Atomic bomb detonation at White Sands. A complicated table of fallout factors. Plume of greatness.

Or how to solve for survival.

2. *Zongide'en*, Be Brave.

Another partial differential equation. Let's say a corporation proposes a mine. Variables include Tyler Forks. Bad. Potato. Rivers. A 22-mile, 22,000-acre strip of land. Jobs. *Maanomin.* Open pit. Exceptional or outstanding resource waters. Legislation. Iron oxide. Fish. Blasting and pulverizing. New legislation.

The functions depend upon the continuous variables. Fluid flow, for example. And changing laws. Somewhere along the granite line, someone enters. Let's say they have put down one life and taken up another: the solution of the PDE.

Warriors (walleye, Indian, new-age) face arbitrary functions. Changing laws. Guards. Guns. If the life is stretched over two points. It vibrates. We cannot measure that vibration in this generation. We can sing it, or make it into light.

Oscar Mireles Poet Laureate of Madison, Wisconsin

History Lesson

My mother Elisa
was picketing outside
the cattle car trains
that were quietly lined up
to deport Mexican nationals
from Minneapolis Minnesota
in the 1920s
Yes, it was her
and three other women,
my Aunt Juanita and two friends
Carmen and Josie Flores
they were afraid to hold up the picket signs
that protested the mass deportations
yet were more afraid
worse things would happen
if they didn't do anything
A local policeman warned them
it would be best if they left
otherwise he would be forced
to take action
but they stood there
waving their picket sign
like a flag
as the last train
fell into the sunset

Rob Hardy Poet Laureate of Northfield, Minnesota

The Arc

The Edmund Pettus Bridge rises in a long arc
a hundred feet above the Alabama River.
On Sunday, the seventh of March, 1965,
the men and women marching out of Selma
couldn't see until they'd reached the top of the arc
the violence waiting for them on the other side.
They thought they saw death waiting
in the wall of billy clubs raised to block the road ahead.
But the marchers followed that descending arc,
still believing it would bend toward justice.
Sometimes we seem to have come so far,
to have risen near the height of history's moral arc,
only to descend. But we keep moving forward.
We come from different places and different faiths,
to live together in this city of bridges, where the land
arcs upward on either side of a moody river,
dreamed into this sacred space by a man
who believed in brotherhood, who believed in justice,
who believed that we would all join hands
and walk together into the promised land.
Dr. King understood that belief is a bridge
to carry us from where we are to where we want to be.
To get there, we still have to rise up and march.
The arc of the moral universe still needs the weight
of people standing together to make it bend.

Mary Weems Poet Laureate of Cleveland Heights, Ohio

"A Piece of American History"

George Zimmerman's description of
the gun he used to kill Trayvon Martin

Murder, Murder most foul.
News reporter's eyes dim as she talks

picture of the gun is shown
it looks used and dull
as a dead face

I smell blood in the body
before it is spilled
innocence and skittles
innocence and skittles

I am still as a breezeless summer night
anger leaves footprints
that follow Trayvon walking home
listening to God's trombone

I read "The starting price is five thousand
dollars" wonder how this amount compares
to the Black lives killed since Trayvon
without anyone being found guilty
of a crime.

Karen Kovacik Indiana Poet Laureate

Adagio

after Tranströmer

This morning I rip out forty flawed rows
of a beloved scarf. The unraveling

makes the yarn loops quiver. This span
that would have warmed your neck

surrenders in quick breaths. Last night
four horsemen bloodied the electoral map.

Now I again cross my needles,
find the rough pulse of the yarn.

How small the future is: a poke,
a wrap, then slipping off.

The slowest of music, this adagio:
blue notes climb and descend

the cryptic staff of a wool concerto,
my only flag. It signals: "We contest."

Knitters in every language twist and lift.
It's the quietest revolution.

Wendy Vardaman Poet Laureate of Madison, Wisconsin

mend in progress

fix | mend | repair | restore | darn | heal | overhaul | service | patch | piece | rehabilitate | renew | stitch | square | correct | right | resolve | amend | recover | ameliorate | revamp | knit | recondition | refit | refurbish | rejuvenate | rectify | rebuild | reconstruct | connect | balance | tune | rivet | zip | accommodate | adjust | renovate | modify | make do | revise | alter | help | recuperate | improve | reclaim | treat | remedy | palliate | attend | do up | soothe | weld | hook | resuscitate | revive | salve | revivify | regenerate | reconcile | reanimate | harmonize | dress | conciliate | doctor | fasten | join | link | secure | tie | unite | weave | assemble | rally | save | reclaim | bridge | rebuild | suture | solder | button | transform

Zora Howard New York City Youth Poet Laureate

Red White and Blue Seuss

One youth
Two youth
Our kids
Uncouth
Skin brown
Face down
Hands up
Black brute
Your hood
My hood
Face slammed
Car hood
Cop cars
Stay parked
Your block
My block
Streets like
Land mines
Black op
Men marked
Law stop
Law frisk
Law strike
Leave scars
Law just
Law kill
Law will
Walk still
Tell him

Scold him
Black boy
Doctrine
Five O
Hunt us
Target
Practice
Young
Defenseless
Labeled
Reckless
Light begets
Us fire won't
End us

Carla Christopher Poet Laureate of York, Pennsylvania

A System Cannot Fail

If I don't break the law,
maybe they won't kill me.

If I don't steal cigarettes,
sell cigarettes,
carry weapons,
carry toy weapons,
carry Halloween costume weapons,
cell phones that bulge a pocket like a weapon,
pill bottles that curve my hand
like a hand that probably wants to,
or might have once held at one point,
a weapon

If I promise not to defend myself against their weapons,
maybe they won't kill me.

If I don't drink liquor,
or soda with my skittles
If I don't eat my words before spitting back
the injustice I'm choking on
I ... STILL ... can't ... breathe

If I don't breathe,
maybe they won't kill me.

Or maybe no matter what I do
they will come for me,
through the wires of my cell phone,

through the vaccine-filled needle,
through sentencing and prosecution,
through protection from indictment,
through the ghosts of Tuskegee,
through the slice of a knife
dividing my piece of American pie
into a revisited 3/5th compromise

If you can kill me, and it only counts some of the time
does it not dehumanize me
completely?

I am a Black woman

and since that dug my grave
the day my mother gave me life,
at least let me hold that

and drag it like a nigger chained
to the back of a rough road riding flatbed.

I WILL riot
in my mind
and in my lines
and in my ideas—until
the matrix overloads
and my rioting explodes into the streets,
crumpling metal and shattering the glass
of soul eye windows
and double-pained ceilings,

until the heat from my rage incinerates page
and screen and stage

and my meaning rises
like a sword wielding phoenix from Biblical ashes

I will take
The Tower
down.

Carla Christopher Poet Laureate of York, Pennsylvania

Reclaimed

My afro is a hipster halo
mimicking the sun,
my dashiki another sneaky reference
to the Black Butterfly
I have become
since discarding the sticky chrysalis
of a monochromatic existence—
my colors run unchecked
through finish lines and pearly gates
I am Heaven
's gold streets
I am Oya, sister and life mate
of Chango
I dance with fire and rule the winds
and I go
wherever I please, these feet
tap dance to the rhythm of destiny
Ease on down,
    ease on down . . .
skin so rich and golden brown
desert and soil fight to claim me
but I am
       still The Sun's.

Joel Lipman Poet Laureate of Lucas County, Ohio

not telling the truth

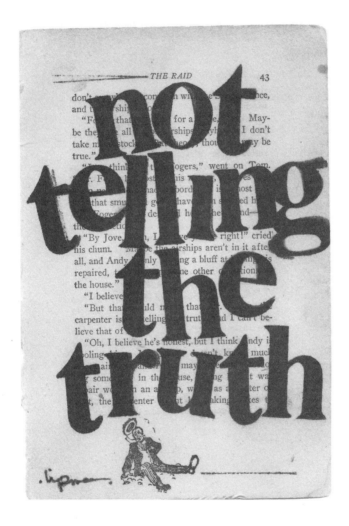

UNITE

"Call a friend or coworker. Organize allies from churches, schools, clubs, and other civic groups. Create a diverse coalition. Include children, police, and the media. Gather ideas from everyone, and get everyone involved."

Sacred Stone Camp

140 years after Little Big Horn,
after gold hungry prospectors
trespassed onto Lakota land
in violation of the Treaty of Fort Laramie,
new oil hungry corporations
threaten to repeat that history—
repeat the violation of tribal sovereignty
repeat brutality toward Native people
repeat disregard for the valor of earth
the sacredness of the resources of this planet
the waters that give us life.

> When our waters are threatened,
> *I stand with Standing Rock.*
> When tribal treaties are disregarded,
> *I stand with Standing Rock.*
> When sacred sites are desecrated,
> *I stand with Standing Rock.*
> When armed militia mace peaceful protestors,
> *I stand with Standing Rock.*

Moving oil makes money—spilled oil contaminates water.
When 783 million people do not have access to clean water,
when 3,300 ruptures or leaks of crude oil and liquefied natural gas
have occurred on U.S. pipelines in the last six years,
we do not need another precarious pipeline.
The Lakota People will not become rich
from oil passing through their lands—
the Missouri River is their wealth.

In the Dakota plains the people of Standing Rock
do not need the prophesied Black Snake
slithering false promises of energy independence—
the ageless force of prairie winds is power.
If the Dakota Access Pipeline is too dangerous for the populations of Bismarck
it is too dangerous for the Native people of Standing Rock.

When we are not equal under the law,
I stand with Standing Rock.
When the gate price of oil bankrupts our future,
I stand with Standing Rock.
When the fossil fuel agenda bulldozes dissent,
I stand with Standing Rock.
When Indigenous nations come together for Water,
I stand with Standing Rock.

When Indigenous nations gather
to sing, dance, and pray,
we don't need rubber bullets shot point blank
we don't need cavalry history repeated.
At a peaceful protest by Water Protectors
we don't need attack dogs
we don't need faces maced
we don't need women locked in cages.
We need energy justice
we need a leader who says stop
a judicial system that says stop—
stop illegal digging
stop penalizing the poor
stop ignoring climate change
stop fracking
stop desecrating sacred sites
stop endangering our waters.

When Indigenous Nations
from the Sami to the Sarayaku
have sent delegations to Sacred Stone Camp
to stand with Indigenous Water Protectors,
where do you stand?
I stand with Standing Rock.
When Indigenous people are
4 percent of the population,
but stand as protectors
for more than 80 percent
of the world's biodiversity,
where do you stand?
I stand with Standing Rock.

Rob Hardy Poet Laureate of Northfield, Minnesota

My Mother's Pussy Hat

On Monday, an ice storm postponed
the Martin Luther King celebration.
Ice coated the streets and the sidewalks.
There was no firm footing anywhere.
Overnight, the rain turned to snow
and the world went suddenly white.
On Tuesday morning, I cleared the ice
from the sidewalk in front of the house,
because this is how we do things
in a cold climate: we give ourselves hernias
so that others won't break their necks.
A sidewalk reminds me that the borders
of our lives are porous, that to tend
our own small frontage on democracy
we must take on the burden of strangers,
and put our backs into the work.
I spent the whole week wondering how.
On Friday afternoon, a dense fog rose,
too much like the ghost of something
we had left to die. In spite of the darkness
and unsteady hands, my eighty-year-old mother
stayed up all night knitting herself a hat. All night
it grew from its long umbilicus of yarn,
taking the shape of something
both pantherine and gynecological.
When Saturday dawned, pink and hopeful,
my mother's pussy hat was one
of millions, as if with enough pink yarn
women could knit a whole nation back together.

Carson Borbely Ann Arbor Youth Poet Laureate

sophia tells me

sophia tells me
that they got the one dimple in their face because when they were little,
they had a gash so big
in their right cheek it had to be stitched up, and that's the way it healed
—concave. there's nobody I'd rather unmap myself to
here, in the basement of the michigan league, which looks like the future
if the future were ugly.
sophia and I compare notes on the way we
and others have left permanent scrapes
on our bodies. they show me the place that their ear,
when sliced off by a bad, sharp
fall, was stitched back together, overlapping. it is the first and only time we
have ever touched.
They say *here, feel!* and I run my finger and thumb
over the place it was sewn on, feel its sloppy thick next to the
rest of the velvet. I show them the burn
on the back of my hand, scar on my knee from climbing straight into
concrete. I show them my forearms, tilt them forward like seesaws so the
nicks will catch the light.
Overlapped, tiny cross-stitches
of skin re rifted. like fault lines in reverse.
I say *but I don't do that anymore.* they say *can you still see it?* and point to the
edge
of their own scar, farther up on the wrist. they say *I did it because
I wanted my dad to notice. I did it because I wanted to see what it would feel
like.* I think about rachel, who in the 7th grade
used a paperclip, and alexa, who in the sixth
used a lighter, there are things that hurt so bad
we want them to hurt on the outside too, or that's how the psychology

27

seems to go. all I know is my mind can bend backwards, stoop
to this, but nothing will make the brain
short circuit and fizzle quite like the body can, zap like spit
on an iron, but our bodies have a threshold
for pain
and we want to see it.
it's stuck in my head: *I want someone
to notice*. I am thirteen and for the first time, bleeding, patched
skin at the cushion
of my arms and I raise my cellphone camera
to take a picture. there is pain,
like this, that I want to externalize. the body is its own defective eraser
and leaves its pink smudges behind
always.
our abrasions
belong to us, and here, we want them,
here, with my finger on their ear,
their dimple out, sideways, gritty, sunny,
there is no sympathy, no mention of phase,
we sit, starting at marks of our body's continual/repeated forgiveness,
grins and new skin like tissue paper where blood used to be. my mom
taught me,
in italian, there is one word for all of it—*cicatrice*. every disfigurement is met
with the same word, tongue cluck,

and handmade salve.

Cavana I. O. Faithwalker Poet Laureate of Cleveland Heights, Ohio

Evangelist

It's eleven a.m.
there's a dude at my door.

"Hi I'm from the Art museum."
"Huh. Where your car at son?"

"We're down the street I walked."

It's July in Cleveland
hot and muggy. "Ok?"
I say squinting glaring.

"Have you been there recently?"
"Naw, son" I spit, staring
not moving a hair.
I been in front of a fan
in the dark, shades drawn
to keep out the sun
It is unforgiving
I'm hot. My back is burning.
My face . . . hot, my feet sting.
My fingernails are hot.
My fan's air, sweltering
"The museum's free."
I wish I was free, I think.

"Here's information on
programs . . . galleries."

29

I'm inferno hot and drunk
and nauseous, hungover
my eyes burn and are wet
from crying and sweat.
I am mad tired. Po Po
wouldn't let me go
till about three a.m. or four.

I defend myself from
dude here with the screen door
hand on the handle keeping
me balanced. False secure.
Left hand rubbing sweat around
On my bare chest and stomach.

"It's a world of great art
for everyone," he says
handing me brochures 'bout
African galleries.

"What? A world of great art?"
Not for Sonny shot dead.
His life for mine at A-Rab's.

Lyrics run through my head:
 "I'm junior high with a B plus grade.
  At the end of the day I don't hit the arcade . . ."

I am lonely scared
damned, tired, and angry.
Wish these would pour out of me.
Like this sweat there are rivers
of scared rivers of lonely,
rivers of angry inside of me.

"Worlds of great art for everyone."

"For everyone?" I ask.

Hell must be like this July day
its heat ever present.
It must be this lonely.
It must be this sad.
Twenty-four seven scorched!
I push open the screen door
surveying concrete streets
not missing Africa
I ask,
"Y'all have air conditioning?"

Rob Rolfe Poet Laureate of Owen Sound, Ontario

Heat

on this day
clouds of
dust swallow

dozers trucks
loaders
and diggers

you can sip
water or
you can pray

for a breeze
it makes
no difference

work goes on
one load
after another

Rob Rolfe Poet Laureate of Owen Sound, Ontario

The Hole

the people up
top don't
think about us

working down
in the hole
he said they

all flush their
toilets but
if we're down

here changing
their shitter
pipe man it's

an open sewer
it lets out
in our hands

Meredith Holmes Poet Laureate of Cleveland Heights, Ohio

The Real World

I was an English major, plus I lack
the armor essential to survival
in this machine tool town that spits spring sleet
and sex-segregated help-wanted ads.
Job-wise, Cleveland gives me the cold shoulder.
I'm alone here—no Sunday-dinner aunts
gamely tossing a knotted rope across the age gap,
asking, "how's the apartment, how's the job?"
No sisters to gossip, dish, and shop with.
It's two days hard rowing from the warrens
where I apply for work to the chapel
of trees where my parents wait, still bullish
on my bachelor's paying its good-job
dividend, as theirs did so long ago.

Karla Huston Wisconsin Poet Laureate

Nogales, Arizona

Because I am not foolish, I have the skin of a saguaro

that has spent its life with raised arms.
Inside this spear, I am hollow.

I cannot tell when a crow reaches in and exposes

the atoms of my ribs. Sometimes
a snake will carry gold into my center.

Or the yellow tears falling on the dry floor

begin to trick each other out of their drifting hair.
All the men I have known have been swallowed by fog

and the stars teetering on mountains at night.

Howard D. Paap Poet Laureate of Bayfield, Wisconsin

Raising the Flag

Several years ago for the first time in nearly a century, the new Red Cliff flag was raised on its own pole in front of the Bayfield Public Elementary and High School where today approximately 80% of the student body is made up of Ojibwe students.

This is a time for flags
Carried high by tight-fisted crowds.
Today flags sometimes shout
As loud as funeral shrouds.

Old Glory, you of the red, white, and blue,
Still rise to be honored and praised
But in Bayfield, Wisconsin, in front of the school
Another flag was raised.

To stand beside your colors,
A cloth of a different sort,
Rose on its shiny new pole,
While an ancient drum loudly beat its report.

This is the flag of the Ojibwe
Who on the Red Cliff Reserve reside.
Today its silence so loud
Will beside your glory abide.

For a new time has arrived
All across the land

No more to be motioned aside,
Now to proudly stand.

A flag of a different nature,
Its stripes of colors true.
Yellow, black, red and white,
The four directions, their sacred hue.

Its canton holding the original clans
Still leading the people on their way,
Now atop this flagpole
Those forebears are here to stay.

As they have from the beginning
High above to tell of their pride
These flags together so fly,
Make their stand, side by side.

Kimberly Blaeser Wisconsin Poet Laureate

Bawaajige

Whispers through my tributaries—
crane voices and stale pow-wow jokes,
Native tragedy and the "great white road."
I won't cliché you, betray you
with the spent hopes of language.

I am the mirror of your indecision:
Your legs are clan longing
and the echo of honor song beats,
your hands the arithmetized remnant
the treaty-tamed blood formula
of civilized greatness.

Rich man, poor man,
Beggar man, thief.
Somewhere in the fray of the tweeted everyday
Doctor, lawyer
Indian Chief.
we parse and compute identity
in columns of the colonized.
Tinker, tailor—
Halfbreed maker.

Now I am the whisper of a whisper
of old crane voices calling
loud, lusty, and long, the Echomakers
calling across captured ledger marks
like Marion prisoners drawing spirit lines

of imagined motion, riding the regalia of horse nations
overruling simplest computations of victory.

Remember you are the tributaries
the many branchings of tribal nations;
you are the blood passage of belonging.
Do not debate this.

I am not made of bones and teeth.
The fibers of my willow hair
cannot be dissected or carbon dated.
You are not made of Xs and Ys.
Your name is not a formula
or test tube fantasy.
You are the misspelled prescription
written to save the Santa Maria from oblivion.
You might debate this.

The spark of Anishinaabeg stars
the Ponca flame, amber and ancient
ignite the obsidian memory of tribal fires:
The burning wolf eyes of clan brothers
the sweet sage scent of hand drum sisters
the hawk cry of hunters,
the partridge drum and turtle rattle songs
the porcupine quill becoming
of our intricately embroidered lives.
You are the blood passage of belonging.
Do not debate this.

Joyce Sutphen Minnesota Poet Laureate

I Say Amen

When I see a woman
and she's carrying a
baby in her arms, or
she's holding an infant-
seat like an egg-basket,
or she's pushing a stroller,
or there's a car-seat wedged
into the grocery cart
which she's moving down
the aisle as the baby starts
crying, or when I see her
walking in the park, following
the child who runs across
the grass to the swings and is
already shouting "Push me
Mommy!" or she is bent
down, tying shoe-laces or
looking for the penny or the
crayon or a piece of the
puzzle, or when I see her
pulling the child into
her lap at the doctor's
office, reading the waiting
room's stories quietly into
his ear, or when she gets up
from her chair, sighing as
she pulls her dancer from
the edge of the pool or
the ledge along the stairs
or when she has to carry
him out and he's screaming

"No Mommy! No!" Or when
she's standing outside of the
auditorium, swaying
to the music she can
no longer hear, or when she
goes out in the middle of
the wedding with a trail
of baby's tears slipping
over her shoulder like a
scarf, when she's taking
the very breakable,
very valuable item
out of his hand,
when she pries the book
away just as a page
is about to be ripped
in two, or when she sees
him put the bottle-cap
into his mouth and pops
it back out with a neat
flick of her finger, or
When she zips up the coat
and wraps a scarf around
twice, tucking the ends in
behind the small head and
leans down to kiss the child's
cheek and send her into
the world, when she does I
say I know, I say amen.

Laren McClung Poet Laureate of Bucks County, Pennsylvania

For Ibrahim Qashoush

They found you like a river stone
in the Orontes where the people fished
you out. & like oil on water
you take the tint of all colors.
Now a streetwise nation wakes,
thousands on the Brooklyn Bridge,
down Broadway, Cleveland,
L.A., on the lawn of the Capitol
jailbreaking our jobs & mountains,
our houses foreclosing or falling down.
There's no due process to undo
a quarter-century of bankers
clapping the beat of a pop tune,
lost to the blindfold of interest.
Listen. They're singing your song
in the square, old & young, a voice
wading out where the cameras can see.

Joel Lipman Poet Laureate of Lucas County, Ohio

Calligraphy

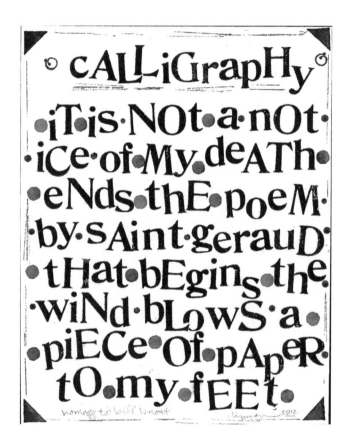

SUPPORT
VICTIMS

"Let victims know you care. Support them
with comfort and protection."

Kimberly Blaeser Wisconsin Poet Laureate

Regarding the Care of Homeless Children

Seven decades later I trace your *Table X*
easily imagine names of the studied,
Maymie Ellen Bunker, John E. Antell,
Nookomis, Nimishoomis,
those who shelter homeless children—
children of legitimate birth
children born out of wedlock
non-members of family.
With appropriate scientific distance
you count abinoojiinyag—
children with *both parents dead*
children with *one parent dead.*
You wonder why *private homes*
should keep these fledglings?
Depression era White Earth Reservation,
legally adopted
adopted "Indian way"
we call them cousins.

Among the *One Hundred Fifty*
Chippewa Indian Families
on the White Earth Reservation in 1938
you catalogue types of houses—
seventy-one tar-paper shack families,
seventy-one frame-house families,
eight rehabilitation house families.

All italicized words are taken from Sister M. Inez Hilger's *Chippewa Families: A Social Study of White Earth Reservation, 1938.*

Your neat columns total incidence—
64 homes sheltering children,
regardless of their type of house, sheltering
78 non-members of family.

Yes, blessed is the fate
of those your *Table X* calls *homeless.*
Chippewa children
brought to live with relatives
taken in as members
by mutual agreement
braided into families
into *tar-paper shacks—*
homes not considered *adequate*
by accepted housing standards.
(Very few of the Indian homes,
you explain, are *considered adequate.)*
And owners of substandard
Indian houses do not qualify
for *aid-to-dependent children funds.*

Still those gathered in my bevel-edged photographs
extended families who fished, trapped, hunted and gardened
who followed seasons then years of subsistence *poverty*
regularly took in new members.
Their *inadequate,* drafty, and over-crowded houses
in Lengby and Naytahwaush,
these substandard structures become safe ground
lodges, dens, nests.

And when you summarize findings
regarding the care of homeless children,
Sister Inez your language shrugs
shakes its head, puzzled, as it concedes

the odd futility of this analysis.
The decision to *shelter* these children
grandchildren
nieces
non-family members
to keep them among the community
stitching them in like beads
in a woodland design
holding close the floral hearts of children
was *not . . . related to housing.*

Rick Kearns Poet Laureate of Harrisburg, Pennsylvania

Tecoani and Alejandro

On September 26, 2014, Mexican police seized 43 students and allegedly delivered them to gang members who killed them, burned their bodies and left some of the remains in a garbage dump. The students, many of whom were indigenous, are known as the Ayotzinapa 43. Alejandro Mora Venancio was one of the 43, from the municipality of Tecoanapa. In Náhuatl: Tecoani means "tiger" and apam means "in the river."

tiger in the river
smells charred bones
in the garbage pile
someone
is lying

tiger swims away
men with machines
bone ash floating
everywhere.

garbage pile
is full today
martyr's boneyard
tiger in the river

executioner
in the palace

someone is dying

I am Alejandro
the swimming tiger
is my protector now.

The tiger in the river
is not another trickster
from the north
he knows who killed me

the tiger in the river
knows about the
executioner in the palace
the tv toadies
the men with masks
the men with helmets

my tiger in the river
is waiting
it's
lunch
time

Aliki Barnstone Missouri Poet Laureate (grew up in Bloomington, Indiana)

Monochrome Prison

I walk my dogs, who are jubilant smelling
winter air. I'm grim. Strive to keep my health.
Gray wind irritates my face, and I chide
myself for not perceiving the design
of tree branches as lovely—black lace fans
opening in sky. I'm free to choose. Maybe
the weight of the news makes my muscles feel
weary with age. After twenty-two years,
Tyrone Hood, a black man wrongly convicted,
was released from prison. The court that judged
he murdered sentenced him to fifty years,
"despite serious doubts about his guilt
and strong evidence pointing to another
perpetrator." When asked "how does it feel
to walk free?" he spoke of the joy of colors.
Twenty-two years of monochrome: black bars,
white walls, the guards' gray uniforms. "I haven't
seen red—only on TV . . . and when I
first saw red, I stared and stared even though
it was a vending machine or something."

Karen Kovacik Indiana Poet Laureate

Your Neck: A History

tankas for Eric Garner

From snaps to buttons
and tee shirts to pressed collars
you grew up and out,
clipping on a wide blue tie
to sing in the children's choir.

"Protect your throat, son,"
she'd say, when November winds
turned sharp. Stink of Vicks.
Mustard plaster. Scarf you'd twirl
and loop to keep your lungs safe.

Tight airways: you'd puff
your inhaler, take that cloud in
your mouth, your body.
A holy ghost would enter
your lungs' church and open you.

Rented tux, bow tie
crisp at your throat. Mama said,
"Just breathe, teddy bear."
Then preacher and choir lit up:
you and Pinky stung with rice.

Diaper at your neck,
you burped your newborn princess,

fitful miracle,
her hiccups a grasshopper's
you could coddle and quiet.

Transmission fluid
splashed your clavicle, axle
grease you wore like gloves,
till the fumes shut down your lungs,
and you escaped with your life.

Six children to feed,
you worked in the New York parks,
spading bulbs, grafting
saplings, but all that flowering
pinched the branches of your breath.

Yes, you sold loose smokes
fifty cents apiece. A "crime"
against capitalism, true,
but not like firing a Glock
at first graders or teachers.

Just before your death,
you broke up an angry fight.
Swords into ploughshares:
they nicknamed you Peacemaker.
You wedged your neck between fists.

Your last words haunt us:
"I can't breathe." At our die-ins,
Berkeley to London,
on sidewalks, basketball courts,
we testify with our breath.

Rebecca Zseder Mississauga Youth Poet Laureate, Ontario

Nameless

There was a room.
Walls, invisible to her curiosity.
Light seeping through stained glass made art of her eyes reflective of the innovation she saw
every time she opened them.
Reflective of all she could create.
The girl stood in the centre, too big for its construction.
Her arms made avalanche of the walls by her side,
Her feet dipped into the foundation,
And her head created the sunroof never seen in the blueprint.
She was far too big for confinements' definition of freedom.

There is a room.
Walls, two by two pushed together to make four.
Dimly lit by disaster.
The girl sits in a corner.
Stained glass reflective of shattered stability,
Arms too weak to stretch, legs too weak to hold the weight of this much
Someone else.
Love is a rabid thing when it is sickly.
It's easy to say that you are hard to love but hard to see how easily
it comes to some.
To one.
To the one who dares enough to change you.
Isn't it funny how sinfully similar the words 'dare' and 'care' are?
Isn't it funny how butterflies manifest themselves into excitement when
their food is sweet enough?
Isn't it funny when they stop telling you to run?
She never understood how it became possible to need someone like
nourishment but all the while feel as though she is the one being consumed.

Maybe this is what love is, thought she.

She thought a lot.

She used to think a lot before his hologram kept stealing her pencil.

She doesn't write anymore.

Thinks more about how to soften the sharp edges as not to make her puzzle piece unfittable.

Thinks more about how to make sure he fits comfortably.

Bites the sheets of maybe it'll be over soon;

The sheets of as long as he says he loves you.

She stares blankly into the holes left where his colossus used to fit,

Wonders what the outside world might look like now,

Too into herself and waiting for him to think up imaginings of what the real 'real world' might be.

She grows into herself.

Too small now to see anything but space around her.

Spends her time finding the right ways to fill it with him.

Spends her time the ways to fill it with him.

Spends her time finding the ways to fill him.

She let her wall down like failed barricades make way for crusades and is more white face than First Nation now.

She without he becomes a snake without purpose but bitterness and absence

And she doesn't know how to fill a mirror anymore.

Because even the word 'she' is filled with more of him than herself.

She had learned how to be filled by men even before she had

become a woman.

She had fought against it and did well so long as no one fought back.

He knew everything about her now.

He always had a way of learning the things about her that she failed to admit to herself.

Or maybe he just had a way of inventing a her in replacement of the one too complex to win against.

He just had a way of flipping her creation upside down and painting his interpretation visible.

He just had a way of making it feel like love.

Mary Weems Poet Laureate of Cleveland Heights, Ohio

Gray Note

I'm watching sky
through window
as verdict's announced
words so familiar
I hear the last time
they were said.

Sky begins to gray
sun drops like a weight
until everything looks like smoke
in a room full of people
talking about judge who decided a Black man's killing
was justified
even though he couldn't breathe
let alone resist.

William Trowbridge Missouri Poet Laureate (born in Chicago, Illinois)

Mercy

found poem based on 1998 interview of a Lithuanian
rifleman in Einsatzgruppen B from 1939–45

Nobody told us what our duties would be.

They just trucked us in one morning.

We only knew our destination when we got there.

It was a military secret.

It was some little town.

I forgot its name.

All the Jewish men were off at war.

Only old folks, women, and children remained.

They were the people we were ordered to kill.

It was shoot or be shot.

The gunners were side by side along the pit with the Jews in it.

We didn't shoot the Jews on the edges.

We killed them after they were forced to lie down in it.

We shot the adults first, then the children—

so the parents wouldn't have to see their children die.

They were brave.

They never screamed or begged.

They lay down, ready to die.

They all had the Star of David on their backs.

To avoid being beaten, they didn't resist.

We'd shoot the nearest victim.

We barely moved the rifle, the person was so close.

We fired two or three bullets.

We tried to aim accurately.

One Jewish man pointed to his chest so we'd aim at it.

I shot him there.

If I'd have only wounded him, he'd have suffocated under the others.

We had to shoot the children dead, or they'd have died by suffocation.

We used incendiary bullets.

They burnt the clothes.

The burnt smell was everywhere.

The older children knew their fate.

They lay down in the pit.

The little ones tried to crawl over to their dead parents.

They crawled on all fours.

The Germans kept the pits surrounded.

They didn't shoot: they supervised.

The Lithuanian soldiers had to shoot the Jews.

German soldiers took photos.

The Germans brought POWs from the camps nearby.

The POWs poured disinfectant on the bodies and shoveled earth over them.

After the execution, German officers walked on the bodies and used their pistols to shoot the people still alive.

Someone asked what I'd say now to a child whose parents I killed.

I don't know.

The little ones . . .

I'd tell them, "there there."

Barbara Buckman Strasko Poet Laureate of Lancaster County, Pennsylvania

Esperancia

At five she was selling food in Haiti,
no time for school, too much hunger
to take care of and now what she misses
about her country is the swimming.

In Argentina a year later there was no safe
passage to school for children of her color.
On the way, she explained *you could be taken.*

She screamed at a man in the market
when he did not pay. She yelled in her
Creole Spanish and the police nearly took
her away *to the place they take you.*

Now at age seven she tells me in soft-spoken English
the memory of her father who was taken and cut,
and when he ran up the mountain out of breath
he sent his family away to the airport, carrying nothing.

She begins to read the book about seasons—
English the language in which she tries to
decipher words, each letter a struggle, each picture new.
To know so little but really know so much . . .

She wants to return to Haiti, to the sun,
and to the many colored fruits of her market.
In three languages, she dreams of swimming.

Rob Rolfe Poet Laureate of Owen Sound, Ontario

No Details

drawn to this
stretch of
the forest she

slipped alone
into its
craggy interior

she's a victim
without
a story already

those who love
her will
be grieving

the police
have released
no details

Norbert Krapf Indiana Poet Laureate

The Potter's Hand

for Jody Naranjo, Santa Clara Pueblo

When I tell you
the story of how
the policeman pulled

his gun & pointed
it into our son's
hysterical face while

we screamed from
the balcony a few
feet away in

the direct line
of fire as six
other squad cars

circled our place
& sirens ripped
apart the peace,

"Don't shoot,
don't do it,
don't shoot,

he's our son,
our son, our son,
we can calm

him down," your
hand that shapes
clay into a pot

reaches out to
mine that writes
the poem & you

say you feel
what we felt,
you are the mother

of three daughters,
the mother, the mother
of three daughters,

& we are joined
as one family
in one story

that crosses over
ancient battle lines
& compassion passes

from the potter's
to the poet's
loving hand.

Russell Thorburn Poet Laureate of the Upper Peninsula, Michigan

I Return to the Surface of the Earth Wearing My Miner's Helmet with Its Third Eye

searching for the men who killed me
who said it was safe to work below
swampy ground on that November day
of the Barnes-Hecker Mine disaster.
As a working man I learned Italian
from the sons of immigrants, my tongue
a shovel and hammer against that rock
of silence we're digging underground.
The mine disaster left my wife a widow,
a young woman of nineteen from Norway,
who wore a flapper's hat shaped like a helmet
and shook the parlor's soul when she danced.

Let me rise and breathe in the cold,
gooselike as a ghost circle chimney smoke
straggling from homes. I was the last man
in the mine to die, to moan my wife's name,
see her round face and golden-brown hair
before breath made slaves of all of us
wanting air before our death in November.
We expected snow over muddy ground,
children to whoop and yell for lost souls
on All Hallow's Eve, for a sea beast to surface
from Lake Superior's gray choppy foam,
for the witch to ride her beanpole
through the chill and cut a silhouette
beside a hungry moon: one day of the year
for those souls to construct a show.

If you see me in my miner's helmet,
those boots with untied laces, susurrate
a surprised prayer, for my third eye searches
for the men who killed me,
those owners who might be washing
their hands of the dead, the men who are
preparing for sleep by stepping into
flannel. Don't listen to the ghostly
creaks of our phantom weight,
tiptoeing forever the same steps
around their beds, all of us
who are dead can't escape
making sounds as we haunt a house.
A carbide lamp's flame from a helmet
flickering upon a wall and our presence
lasts as long as a bad dream when
those bosses find a new sleep position
with a belly flop and cry out names
from the troubles in this world.

I want to remember what it felt
like to be a man with my wife,
watching her toil at English, words
as big as her eyes looking at a son
of a Swedish immigrant, soup warmed
up that afternoon, for me to work
and return home, not expect women
buried in shawls and their revolution
of red eyes. They said it was safe
for fifty-one miners underground,
the deluge of the tunnel
not possible, but our last bulwark
was our big shoulders floating
under broken timber and rock.

Ellie Schoenfeld Poet Laureate of Duluth, Minnesota

Some Things I've Noticed about Jesus

When Jesus fed the poor
he did not ask anyone
to provide proof
that they were sufficiently destitute
to receive the free food.
When Jesus healed the sick
he did not deny care
based on ability to pay,
the rich were not healed
more thoroughly than the poor.
Jesus did not follow a doctrine
of worthy and unworthy poor,
he did not say
only love the neighbors
you already like.
Jesus liked the poor,
he hung out with them,
talked about them a lot—
the poor the poor the poor the poor—
he really did go on and on about them
and none of it was demeaning.
Jesus talked to the rich a lot
about the poor,
encouraged the rich
to give up all of their money
and all of their stuff
to—you guessed it—the poor.
Jesus felt very bad for the rich
because the odds of that camel

getting through the eye of that needle
were pretty slim,
because it looked so likely
that the rich would, in spite of so many
warnings, parables, and examples
keep following their money
and then he and his dad
would have to tell them
to go to hell.

David Jones Philadelphia Youth Poet Laureate

North Star

Death is only a euphemism
For losing a body and gaining a star.
You know
The things they teach you to shoot for?
They shot for me.
Now I'm the light of the world.

Ain't nothing grave about where I am
It's sad how I got here
But I'll make the most of eternity.
I am in it.
Yet, there's no "i" in eulogy or funeral
It was all for you

Stop trying to find the meaning of life in my corpse

A body is a star's casing
Mortality is only skin deep
Death is just a euphemism
So praise be to the bullets that let my light through
An astrophysicist had to view my autopsy
There's something eternal beneath the epidermis.

I am luminescent
Burn too ceaselessly to be fluorescent
Far from evanescent
I'm everlasting
Light of the world don't die out

So stop mourning.
Celebrate me
I am the morning.
Celebrate me.
I am not just another body bodied by injustice.
I am the north star,
Leading you toward a freedom that most don't get before a casket.

damian lopes Poet Laureate of Barrie, Ontario

our home on native land

after Honouring the Truth, Reconciling for the Future, Truth
and Reconciliation Commission of Canada, 2015

the new status
    not status quo
        status symbols
of a mythic past
best before
        blind dates
but our history led
to a different present than this
lie laid low
      pervasive
to read not right
the speech of Sir John A
to the commons in 1883

when the school is on reserve
the child lives with savages
surrounded by savages though
he may learn to read & write
his mode of thought is indian
he is simply a savage
who can read & write
withdrawn from parental influence
they will acquire
modes of thought of white men

not my men yet
an old quote
status quo in 1920
a founding confederation poet
architect of indian affairs
Duncan Campbell Scott

our objective
to continue until
not a single indian
has not been absorbed
into the body
politic

difficult to absorb this politics
comprehend the echoes
of consuming so many peoples
national indigestion of linguicide
as family & culture dissolve
on the tongue
        assimilated to nullify
treaties signed & lands confiscated
obfuscating theft in philanthropy

reaffirmed in my birth year 1969
the White Paper policy perpetuated
the non-status squaw
one drop too many
bound tongues to improve speech
our brutality to overcome their savageness
                    our savage mess

without reservation
we broke our word

stole this land & demand
our victims be silent
& idle
no more

Joel Lipman Poet Laureate of Lucas County, Ohio

BeriBeri

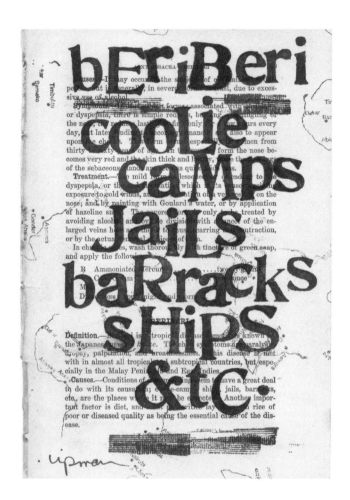

DO YOUR HOMEWORK

"An informed campaign improves its effectiveness."

Donald Hall United States Poet Laureate (lived in Michigan)

Bacteria

Politics has fogged the air of my life. Of course I vote with my New Hampshire grandfather for Democrats, or maybe I merely vote against Republicans. Only once did Wesley Wells neglect to vote Democratic, when the national party ran Al Smith for President. If a Catholic were president, it was common knowledge, the Pope would occupy a wing of the White House. In his whole life, my grandfather never met a Catholic. One time in my life I didn't vote. I've regretted it. I couldn't vote for Hubert Humphrey because he favored LBJ's Vietnam war. I put Nixon in the White House.

The only time I've expressed my politics in a newspaper was 2014.

Back in 2010 a Massachusetts Republican named Scott Brown beat a complacent Democrat to fill dead Ted Kennedy's seat in the Senate. Two years later, when the seat came up in its normal spot, Brown lost the seat to Elizabeth Warren, a notably liberal Democrat. Two years later, in 2014, Scott Brown moved his residence to New Hampshire and ran against an incumbent democratic woman. He was handsome, corrupt, and drove a cosmetic pickup truck. 2014 was the Republicans' Ebola Landslide. The President had assured the people that there would be no Ebola outbreak in the United States, and then to prove him wrong a West African with Ebola flew to Houston and died. A Democratic outbreak! Scott Brown predicted that hordes of Mexican jihadists would crawl into Texas, their prayer rugs saturated with Ebola virus.

He lost. I take credit because of my last poem, three lines I contributed to my local daily.

Get out of town,
You featherheaded carpetbagging Wall St. clown,
Scott Brown!

The Boston Globe reprinted it. Somebody put it on the Internet. It went bacterial.

Tony Pena Poet Laureate of Beacon, New York

Bully Bliss

All the news deemed
by an unfit man to print,
apocalyptic passages
pandering to hateful
lemmings and smudging
an oily film of deception
over our brass tacks,
but the ink is invisible
as he forgets in his fits
of ego that even Lady
Liberty came across
the ocean from France.

Sarah Sadie (Busse) Poet Laureate of Madison, Wisconsin

She Is So Fragile, This Figure, Set Here to Stand

On the re-dedication of the replica Statue of Liberty
Warner Park, August 12, 2012

A gift, inherited from a time when citizens
were blacklisted for belief, and neighbor, friend,
coworker called on to rat each other out,

a time when it was easy, tempting, and even
seemed sensible to fear and to despise.
Likewise, first restored as generations clashed,

arguing a war's reason, a war's cost,
arguing questions of civil rights, how far
they should extend, how far we would extend ourselves.

Those times, not unlike this time. Each era
takes its turn. And so we gather here,
thanks to the unpaid hours of volunteers,

the slow-earned pennies collected by children
in a local elementary school which will, this fall,
with all the other schools, be locked.

When we go home today, Liberty will remain
to occupy this park, holding her torch,
sustaining her puzzles and paradox:

how to be free and indivisible at once?
Let us be generous with each other.
Let us be of good cheer,

that future generations may tell us, as they
restore her yet again, that she eroded
only from the rain, and not from hate. Nor fear.

Joyce Sutphen Minnesota Poet Laureate

Black and White Photographs

This is how he (she, they, it) looked when they
were older (younger, richer) than they are
now. This is how he looked. Something about

the eyes and the way his hands are folded
together, thumb to thumb, four fingers up
and four fingers down. This is how he looked.

And this is the famous writer (*he* was
an actor) when she was meeting a storm
head on, silhouetted by the cloudy

sky, her hair in ropey braids, her earrings
gold as suns, the barest bit of landscape
showing. And this is how the bodies looked—

rotting in the trenches. We do not know
their names, but this is how the bodies looked.

M. L. Liebler Poet Laureate of St. Clair Shores, Michigan

American Psalm: Viola Liuzzo—American Hero

"I don't want to be your hero . . . I just want to fight
like everyone else." —Joe Keefe, "Hero"

I come from a place
Where unspoken heroes
Are born to make a difference
And are never heard from again.

Kevin Stein Illinois Poet Laureate

The Narcissistic Poet's Mad-Lib

The problem with history is I'm *in* it.

I'd prefer my _____ bereft of cop-kills
              furniture item
and videotaped _____ , a retreat from all
                fruit
but retreating. I favor my _____ and newspaper
                              drink
fonted with invisible ink, sans the _____ potion,
                                    nation
post-accident cop waving his _____,
                            body part
"Nothing to _____ here. Move along."
              holiday
For once, a blank _____ needles no heebie jeebies,
                  cutlery
only calm akin to the nothing it _____.
                                verb
Mine transcribe the tabloid's _____ Section,
                              song title
abuzz and abloom, the peskiest of _____
                                  animal
amenable to deep-root _____. If a _____ teeters,
                      exclamation   *flower*
it's the Monarch butterfly, not the _____ citizenry
                                    adjective
whose names stutter-clot _____ consonants.
                          proper name

I'll admit to _____ milkweed, lured by
             -ing verb
the catalytic launch _____ rocketing me outside in,
                    vegetable
the sudden un-handcuffed link of that big _____
                                          circus animal
trundled amid our tenured _____ lounge.
                         toiletry item

Kevin Stein Illinois Poet Laureate

Postcards of the Homefront

1. Anderson, Indiana / 1969

I tried the colors on for size when *Easy Rider*
                    fashioned anti-war decorum,
            stitching the flag to my jeans jacket.
Flash of my neon teenage-brain, humming
                    Four Dead in O-HI-O,
            Make Love Not War!—pledging
allegiance to paisley and good dope.
                    You were a kid, kid—
            warrior of the tribe of certainty,
uncertain of all but that. Your father, veteran
                    of the not-last Great War,
            machine-gunned your parade,
rata-tatting "The flag's no hippie rag."

2. Post 9-11 Trick-or-Treating with My Kids, Kickapoo, Illinois

Bury or burn it? This talk of what to do
                    with the wounded flag
            one month after. How it flapped unstitched
across white-washed porches, waved shredded
                    from the Ford's antenna,
            cracked your lapel pin's cheap Chinese brass.
My jacket, revolution worn once,
                    had moldered amid the kids'
            bedsheet ghosts, hostage
of my father's dust.

On my back the jacket
waves ambivalence
the nodding mommies and daddies
don't deduce. Lost breath—
there in Kickapoo
named for the tribe we gun-nudged west
upon that Trail of Tears—
flag worn upside down
like a country stood upon its head.
I'm talking to you,
the shudder and ash
of what came down
coming down.
Twins, you and I,
fists swung through empty air,
ours the only teeth
to crash
into.

Yolanda Wisher Poet Laureate of Philadelphia, Pennsylvania

the ballad of laura nelson

Laura Nelson was lynched with her son on May 25, 1911, near Okemah, Oklahoma, from a railroad bridge over the North Canadian River. The poem is based on four photographs of the lynching taken by George Henry Farnum.

a. picture of evil #2898

Mama Laura
hangs from the eave
of a bridge
dress like a nightgown
crook in her neck
feigning sleep
bare feet & fingers swollen
with death's whiskey

this is the morning after
the mob stormed the jail
found her dark & vicious
like a coyote cornered on
a Guthrie-guilty road

this is the morning after
she was stretched &
slaughtered by the stampede
made haint
of truss & trestle
made wild in the wind

like a panther prowling
a Guthrie-guilty song

b. picture of evil #2897

bridge like an ark
lined with livewire bodies
ladies with wide hats
parasols & children
like shark teeth
the river's brush
holds their dirty secrets
coiled words gliding
across troubled water
evil themes in the overgrowth
american justice
in its infancy

some dared say
there was a baby
left yonder by the riverside
the birds & bees
& butterflies
pickin out its eyes

c. picture of evil #2894

once
i accused a Boy of stealing
a line of pretty black horses
a line about a book
a book named for a lullaby

sung by a mammy
i accused him of a stealing a line about
a land of unimaginable iniquity

& so his Mother marched
to the Principal's office
pulled my poems from her purse
held them twisted like innards
torn like petticoats
a bunch of river reeds in her hand
bruised with highlighter marks
those scarlet letters
raked between us
with the teeth of pony combs
she said i was a thief of allusions
the Principal called for a moment
of silence

then the Mother
wringing hands & poems
apologized:
"i'm just a bear for my son"
(i'm just a virgin mary for my son)
(i'm just a betsy ross for my son)
(i'm just a rosie the riveter for my son)

i had a little son then
a black-brown watermelon
seed of a boy

& in a moment of silence
i became even more grizzly
the Boy's plagiarized words
became endangered bears

i had skinned
with my eyes

she said that shit to me:
i'm like a bear for my son
& i thought
sister, if you are the bear
i am a cunt like a bear-trap
the worst evil
you can imagine
that bear you thought you saw
that you didn't see
the evil you see
that ruins me
yeah, she said that shit to me
& i went wild inside & it
    has never stopped
      the going wild
        inside

d. picture of evil #2899

how you protect
a Boy from that bridge
how do i protect my Boy
from that bridge
when you are protecting
the bridge with your Boy

i'm going to braid & coat
his little tongue
with the iron edge of truth
the sweetgrass memory of the river

so he'll know those tastes
above all others

you Pilgrim, you Cowboy, you Reader
there is nothing unimaginable about iniquity
this, our land, of iniquity
of tis of thee
on which we bear children
considered burdens
on which we farm barren wombs
of unbearable blackness
in these forests
full of men more terrible
than encroaching bears
looking right
into the camera

George Elliott Clarke Canadian Parliamentary Poet Laureate

The Progress of *Servitude*

One part of *Humanity*
saddled the backs of the other parts,
who ate gruel,
while their riders feasted on sugar—
edible diamonds.

Cane got tapped on three continents
and in the Carib and Indo seas.

Sugar juices fuel th'Americas,
sweeten Europe,
making coffee, tea, chocolate,
digestible commodities.

Gold squeezed from sugar
firms coal mining,
iron works,

guinea circulation.

Sugar throws a railway cross Haiti.

Sugar transfuses blood of (black) Haiti
into once faltering, now gleaming, white banks *de France*.

Slave-grown sugar, turned rum,
pays for "slave pennies,"
Barbados' first coins.

In Brazil, gold sugar goes into gold mines;
white-diamond sugar goes into diamond mines.

Sugar, got from Haiti, transforms to asphalt,
railway steel ties,
even dredged canals,
so British ships and trains and subways
make the world go round Piccadilly Circus.

To get sugar outta New World soil,
Africans get traded for glass beads, guns, trinkets, whiskey,
then herded like cattle aboard vessels.

Slavery equals *Sugar Centuries.*

If the Middle Passage don't drown or disease-to-death most—
tossed overboard like sick horses—
they land on "American," Euro-Zone seaboards
(from which "Indians" have been cleared,
killed off),

then are scoured, de-loused,
shaved, skin oiled,
then measured, graded,

white fingers stuck into their orifices

to test teeth-strength,
or guess at fertility,

labour health,

and then auctioned off
or marketed by "scramble"

(buyers snatching whoever they want),

and, once bought, are branded,
by wrought—hot—iron,

then marched or carted off
to the owner's plantation(s),

while protestors (resisters) are "seasoned"—
i.e., whipped into obedience,
lashed into "good behavior."

["Likely Slaves For Sale"
sold alongside livestock
and dry goods,
brought the buyer:
1—Rice hand, bad eyesight;
2—Good cook;
3—Fair carpenter;
4—Rice hand and blacksmith;
5—Seamstress, infirm;
6—Nurse;
7—Prime Cotton man;
8—Mule-handler (answers to "Bill");
9—Boy ($400 value);
10—Prime girl (named "Honey"; $850 value);
11—Blacksmith (called "Happy," approx. 60 years; $500 value);
12—Studman ("George"; $100 value—likely to run off).]

Soon, the conch shell is blown afore daylight,
and all hands gotta get on their feet
for roll call,

then go, beaten, half-fed, to *Toil*:

This retinue of slaves.

(Cultivating sugar takes muscles, sweat.
Sap spoils lickety-split.
Must be processed inside a day.
Night shifts help.

Boiling sugar requires infernal heat,
So water is gushed on mill roofs
to forbid fire springing up.

Overseers have whips but also emergency machetes:
In case a drowsy slave slips into machinery,
the machete handily lops a trapped hand
or caught foot.)

Everywhere, sugar-financed slaves
clear forests, bush,
build roads and houses,
dig canals and latrines,

and drop down into mines,
to work there,

gettin solid light out the darkness.

[Regina (Saskatchewan) 28 *novembre* mmxiv]

George Elliott Clarke Canadian Parliamentary Poet Laureate

The True History of Jesse Williams*

I.

Skippered fresh from Scotland, the boyish clerk—
too young to enumerate multitudinous sins—
beamed snow-clean, stood lily-upright . . . .

But the sinister fist of Jesse Williams, 43—
ex-slave, Civil War vet, vermin of Texas—

hacked up the kid with a razor,
then whacked 'im with an axe.

The feeble backing for this *Disgust*
was Williams' staggering drunkenness:

Addled, he figured a mercantile *Transaction*
was a *Fraud* perp'd by Adams.

Thus the lad's skull spluttered apart.

A hash cook, extra glowering—
thanks to his twitchy left eye,
Negro Williams staged a no-show of *Industry*;
did not plod after the creeping plough.

Nope. Instead, he dismayed Adams
via hatcheting and cross-hatching *Butchery*,

emphasizing roguish *Dexterity*,

leaving po' boy Adams an abiding ruin—
like wintering trees[†]—

statuesque, but dislimbed.

II.

The scene is Calgary, North West Territories,
Dominion of Canada, 1884:
As disorderly as a market,
the city's as policed as is a cemetery.

(The *Telephone*'s only now on call.)

White dudes jumped on horses—
a stablekeeper passed the posse free reign—
to gallop after Williams—

and "Religious"—
the comical wench Williams dubbed his "wife"—

and deliver both *Spite*.

The lynch mob schemed *un cinquain* of *Slaughter*:
1) "nigger" Williams, 2) two "half-breeds," 3) two "squaws."

The Sarcee lady and buffalo-black dude
trampled snow as they ambled,

and so were custodied—
four miles outta town—
in the Sarcee camp.

The pair faced "blasts of *Magnitude*,"
if they'd not heed
the tenacious facts:

Outmaneouvered & outgunned.

III.

"Judge Lynch" be *de facto* American President.
In Canada, though, darkies
receive a trial and a stalwart *Defence*,

despite their bare-face *Guilt*.

Though men brewed, spewed, dark words,
plotting Williams' black-ass fall
(outside of *Law*),
such caustic *Carnage*
be "Un-Canadian,"
speaketh da Judge.

Still, Williams' trial was taut,
was minstrel-banjo *Minimalism*:

Just one day,
including five mins for the jury
to unanimous their *Bias*.

Even Religious was not—well—faithful,
for she cut loose her "husband,"

while cutting loose a helluva lot of *Damnation*

on his "no-good, no-count, an quite sorry, nigga."

(Williams was, ironically, a bit like Christ:
Abandoned by all
in His last hours.)

IV.

Passing "smoke-browned, picturesque" teepees,
en route to Calgary,
Williams confessed he'd wanted
"grub and coin"
when he slashed stripling Adams into string.

He blamed "vials of violent spirits"
for his "damned vile fix . . . ."

"A drunkard's house
is a merry universe."‡

Said he only needed two six-shooters
to scatter the posse
that lasso'd him.

With perfect *sang-froid* in his cell,
Williams waxed in *Gall*:
succeeded to half-sunder his chains . . . .
Almost busted free!

So, he got shackled down,
and anchored by a 30-pound ball-and-chain.

But the Negro has a demonic composure.

The Negro is *aurum* and *argentums*.

V.

A 16-foot scaffold will uphold *Justice*,
letting Williams dangle,
strangling as he hangs.

That "Black Tower" cannot be escaped
easily.

His hanging will be
weightless *Choreography*.

(The jailhouse preacher lisps 2¢ wisdom
clasped by $10 words.)

Williams pledges he'll see his victim, Adams

(from whom blood flew
as if from hog slaughter),

in Heaven.

[Hull (Québec) 14/7/14]

---

* Cf. Colin Thomson.
† Cf. Plath.
‡ *The Calgary Herald,* April 2, 1884.

James Armstrong Poet Laureate of Winona, Minnesota

Pulling Out

August 19, 2010

That was the summer the war ended—
the other war, and it wasn't exactly over—
some of them would be staying
but most were going
home: soldiers in digi-camo battle dress,
like abstract expressionist
curtains from the '50s, or jigsaw puzzles
(you could see where they'd been put back together),
strapped down in rows in the fuselage
of a C130, or riding the leviathan bed
of an armored Stryker
down highways that started nowhere
and ended nowhere: the desert horizon
like a razor cut on the infinite.

Remember the hand-lettered signs
that hung in our neighborhood, reading
"No Blood For Oil"? (that was
2002—the year of the "smoking gun"
when a bed sheet hung over La Guernica).
But oil is blood, "blood of the earth,
the blood of victory" they said
in 1918, when they ended the War
to End all Wars
and set up the next one.
Ask the Romanians, whose oilfields

were Hitler's Christmas cracker. The growling
Panzer divisions and whistling Stukas needed
the blood of the earth
to shed the blood of men.
Ask the Iraqi divisions who stood with
their hands on the heads
in the heat in front of American tanks
in that other Gulf war,
for that other President
Bush. So this was the end
of summer; like every summer
we came home from vacation and dried out our tent,
flipped through the mail, weeded the garden,
read the newspaper: IT'S OVER, the headline said:
the last Stryker division crossed the frontier.

And on the next page, the dry account
from Superior: a Wisconsin vet
shot his wife, his daughter, his pets
and then put the still-hot pistol into his mouth.

Larry Jensen, Poet Laureate of Owen Sound, Ontario

Burial Ground

When you found bones in your basement
When you found bones in your floor
You surely knew they were bones of ancestors
Bones of those who came before

Deeds of lies, deeds of deception
Ink for blood, blood for gold
The diggers dig and then uncover
The remains and bones so cold

In back yard they kept vigil
Behind curtain you kept watch
They kept fire they beat drums
You make call and lawyer comes

Deeds of lies, deeds of deception
Ink for blood, blood for gold
The diggers dig and then uncover
The remains and bones so cold

*"It is important to understand how First Nation peoples view burial grounds.
To them, their ancestors are alive and they come and sit with them when they
drum and sing.
They did not bury them in coffins, so they became inseparable from the soil.
They are literally and spiritually part of the earth that is so a part of them.
That is one reason why they have such a strong feeling for the land of their
traditional territories—
'our ancestors are everywhere.'*

It is a sacrilege to disturb even the soil of a burial ground. It is an outrage to disturb, in any
way, actual remains." —David McLaren

Deeds of lies, deeds of deception
Ink for blood, blood for gold
The diggers dig and then uncover
The remains and bones so cold

Emilio DeGrazia Poet Laureate of Winona, Minnesota

Visitations

The stranger came from south of all borders,
From a village flooded every spring
When the waters of the Sea of Galilee turn black.
He smelled of garlic, sweat and fish,
And his hair danced like seaweed on his back.

"Let me do this or that for you," he said.
"I'm alone in a doorway looking out.
Let me tell stories to your kids,
Change your motor oil to water
And your water to wine,
And wipe the stains
From the windows of your church."

No, they said no again because
His tongue twisted their words all wrong
And all the carwashers up north
Didn't amount to a hill of beans

And there was no way of seeing
To the bottom of eyes so brown.

Peter Meinke Florida Poet Laureate (born in Brooklyn, New York)

Carina

> America's entering a golden age of faith.
>
> —President George W. Bush

. . . electric stations of the cross bloom like
stigmata in Mississippi as America
loosens its Bible belt for the millennium

and *Verily Verily* amplifies over airwaves:
Behold wise men from the South hawking
balms in the wilderness O Biloxi O

Lynchburg bearing the portable Word
on Wheels to the mobile homeless burning
rubber for Jesus and calories for life everfasting

and 1000 light years away Carina
with its double star winks while pilgrims
in waxy clusters swerve off thruways mounting

toward Jerusalem under the golden arches
singing *Lord I Want To Be A Christian*
Over Ten Billion Saved and counting . . .

damian lopes Poet Laureate of Barrie, Ontario

la mémorial des martyrs français de la déportation

paris, 2011

the guard stumbles in
guttural english
to tell an american
with two canes
that she cannot enter this
place dedicated to the deported
enemies of nazism
who bore the red triangle
of political dissidents
green criminals
blue emigrants
purple religious deviants
pink homosexuals
the brown of the roma here
still called gypsies
the double yellow
of the jewish star
or the black triangle of the asocial
the alcoholics & addicts
vagrants & prostitutes
the mentally delayed
& differently abled

'twenty-six steps' she trips
turning to point slightly softer in french
'c'est trops dangereux

les escaliers
tu ne peux pas passer'
she condescends
'la ministère de la défense
est responsable si tu
                    tombes'

finally strict numbers allow
us to descend the concrete
steps into the hollow tomb
the floor crisscrossed triangles
holding hallow walls
rough without purchase
to the liberty of blue sky
with but two breaks
the stairs & a gate
across to la seine
barred by black metal
spearheads

concealed
a third cleft shrouds
cells of confinement
around a bronze disc
remembering those who
entered the earth

through bars
the unknown black slab
flanked by seventy-six thousand
unlit lights
fewer than three
thousand returned

letters scratched
blood in concrete
speak eloquence of human
deprivation
the names of death
camps made real in
side chambers where
triangular recesses
hold earth & ash
from these places
all these people

ascending in bright sun
our faces burn relief
& once more we light
on notre dame
the beauty & reverence
we ought to grant
each other

Ken McCullough Poet Laureate of Winona, Minnesota

Patriotism

At Wounded Knee
in 1890
the 7th Cavalry
mowed down 300
unarmed Miniconjou Lakota
men, women and children
and 31 of their own
in the crossfire.
26 Congressional Medals of Honor
were awarded for
"conspicuous and gallant conduct"
in this ten-minute "battle."
Yet ever since then
disproportionate numbers
of Lakota warriors
are first to volunteer
to defend this nation
which slaughtered their ancestors
and shattered the Sacred Hoop.

Howard D. Paap Poet Laureate of Bayfield, Wisconsin

Signs of the Times

Today on Lake Superior's Madeline Island, signs in the Ojibwe language
mark significant places. Accompanied with English translations these
signs tell of the Ojibwe people, their historic and contemporary connection with
the island.

Made simply of wood, paint, and words,
The new signs at the town's swimming beach,
In their silence, loudly shout,
Stop and listen while we teach

You, about whose land this was
And in deep ways still remains.
For Ojibwe Country reaches far and wide,
And now, today, as summer's rains

Wash clean these silent signs
Written in Ojibwe, a language old, but today so young.
Its words filled with love for this land
This place from which was suddenly sprung

An admonition to love these waters, this air
The fishes, and all their kin
The plants and winged ones and those of the fur.
Be aware of the world you are living in.

As you step along, in your summer's bare feet
Feeling the earth and seeing these words
Pause to ponder why they are here
These Ojibwe language signs so far, yet so near.

Catch the rhythm and beat
The cadence old
This language of yore
That now speaks so bold.

This is Ojibwe Country
And it's the tribesman's turn,
To stand up front and teach,
While you take notes, listen and learn

That we are one with all
The earth, its waters and winds, our role,
Not the chosen ones as we thought
But only part of the whole.

Listen to these signs
So quiet and clear
Give them your heart,
Lend them an ear.

Embrace this earth and all within
And know you are part
Of its many life forms
Heed these signs and make the start

To love your neighbor,
The life forms all 'round
Listen to this
Ancient tongue's resounding sound.

Join us on this journey
Of life with all
Let us see the day when we
Beckon this language's ancient call.

Joel Lipman Poet Laureate of Lucas County, Ohio

mortality varies

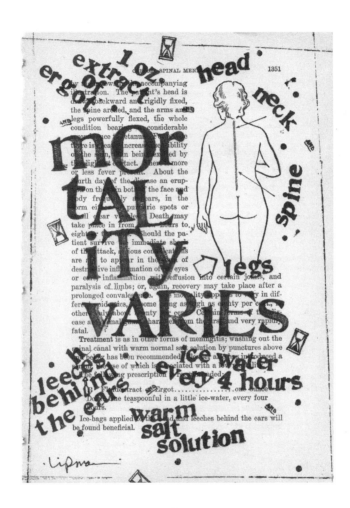

CREATE AN ALTERNATIVE

"Every act of hatred should be met with an act of love and unity . . . Hold a unity rally or parade to draw media attention away from hate."

Carla Christopher Poet Laureate of York, Pennsylvania

Thirty-Six-Thirty

The latitude line between "slave" and "free" states
and Civil War Era slang for a Black person.

He called himself "Sir."
Not boy.
Not dude.
Not thug.
Not hood.
Not coon.
Not jigga.
Not nigger.
Not "nigga."
Not Negro.
Not Colored.
Not Black.
Not "You people."
Not Toby
Not Sam.
Not Tom.
Not Ben.
Not porch monkey.
Not tree-hanger.
Not mud duck.
Not jungle bunny.
Not stove pipe.
Not spook.
Not suspicious person.
Not suspect.

Not P.O.W. (Person other than White).
Not O.B.G. (Original Blue Gums).
Not D.O.A. . . .
walking.

Because again,
and again,
they had taken his name,
he chose
to call himself "Sir."
In itself,
a revolution.

Carla Christopher Poet Laureate of York, Pennsylvania

Why Our Boys Create Their Own Scars: A Mother's Lament

I can't breathe
I can't breathe
I can't breathe
Trayvon Martins wrapped
in hoodies, black boys carry shrouds on their backs
Eternally ready,
fashion has become destiny,
fabric woven into self-fulfilling prophesy,
the enemy is a reaper
in a raincoat with the scissors of Atropo,
severing threads,
leaving heads rolling in the wake, a tidal wave of
blood in the streets
Should I wrap my newborn son in his death sheet
and save myself the trouble of in between?
The fabric of birth and death looks the same,
red stains
against an eternally white foundation

Your head
grows too big for my hands
Your heart
grows too big for my hands
and since I cannot keep you small
I battle teaching you to slouch, slink and crawl
rather than stand
Our attempts at self-protection are too often futile
and I dig 6 foot deep holes

in my 40 acres of land so that I can be ready
to lay you down softly
when your charcoal colored fate demands
I surrender you to the sacrificial plans
of your founding Father.

These black boys,
still walking the street with headphones on
—Turn down for what?—
muffling the sound of gun barrels tapping impatiently
against the aluminum frames of police cars,
windows open and drivers waiting—
I watch my sons become
shadows,
meditating on the many ways they can at least influence
the bridge for their inevitable crossover

Warriors still,
they hold a last melted hunk
of charred dignity
in a clenched fist

Rebelling,
they choose their own scars
and amidst the blood and beauty
they are reborn
and they resist,
if in no other way than by living fully,
by impulse,
in desperate affirmation
that they exist.

Patricia J. Goodrich Poet Laureate of Bucks County, Pennsylvania

Holstein and Stones

The white patches look less like a Holstein heifer; still
they stand out against the ground, reminders of a winter not quite
gone although the sun's angle would have one believe otherwise.

So late a spring even the newscasters ignore the absence
of cherry blossoms in Washington. Without their cheery
distraction, there is no reprieve

from the flurries of bad news—suicide plane crashes, beheadings,
unwelcome alliances, ancient fights over riparian rights
and black underground pools.

This morning I turned on the television
and couldn't stomach the chatter
and went back to bed and slept past later.

Here I sit with my second cup of coffee, chewing on the cud of this day,
trying to write myself to dandelion pastures, like Uncle Ray's
where glacial field stones work their way up each spring,

vital as any bulb, there for my picking—stones
I'd stack and collect, stones Michiganders used to build
homes and chimneys, not so different

from the Berber houses I've visited
in Morocco's Atlas Mountains, half a world away,
although there the bells you hear are of sheep and goats.

And there I would share a glass of green tea with women who spin and weave and drum together, determined to make their own news.

Fred Wah Canadian Parliamentary Poet Laureate

Idle No More: Dec 29/2012

day nineteen is a Saturday here still raining out there
in nono land the codes tumble the parade less idle
each day still the language age quiet in the light
smoke over Victoria Island waiting for the right
grammar to unlock the ladder that connects this world
with the one good words give rise to.

Christopher Bursk Poet Laureate of Bucks County, Pennsylvania

Confiscated Weapons

Which story do you want? Ed Z. asks.
The one I tell the lawyers
or the one nobody wants to hear?
                              In high school
I had no inkling I'd end up in jail
listening to a carbuncular young man read a sonnet
about cutting his father down from the rafters,
and not knowing what to do with the knife
afterwards. Throw it away?
                              Keep to use again?
Ricky Dee has written an ode
in which he can't stop shouting at his mother
as if she's not really dead on the floor,
                              just obstinate.
As a boy I was too busy hurting
to suspect anyone could hurt
as much as I did. I devoted all my spare time to yearning
as if yearning might make me noble,
                              doomed and brilliant.
Everyone in jail has a secret he wants
pried from him, a grief she's doing her best
to live with, account books full of wrongs
                              done each of them:
Nick's competing versions
of what happened the night he killed his father;
Steven's long-winded explanations
of why he was caught in the library,
with his hand in a young boy's pants;

Tiny's quiet misery, Frannie's principled rage;
Mary Ellen's missing trash bag of cocaine.
                    We swap stories,
each of us hoping for a lighter sentence
than we know that we deserve.

Christopher Bursk Poet Laureate of Bucks County, Pennsylvania

Close Your Eyes, I Tell the Men

Close your eyes, I tell the men
but of course they don't.

At first. This is, after all, jail
and you'd would be wise to keep your eyes open

even when sleeping, especially sleeping.
Shut your eyes. Just for a little while!

Nick's staring at me. He's got no other weapons
but his eyesight now

and he's not afraid to use it.
I stare back until even he gets tired.

The intake officer can seize your wallet, shoes,
your *Autobiography of Malcolm X,*

but not the darkness imploding inside your eyelids.
Your mother may have found drugs

more deserving of her attention
than you, your father may have tricked you

into believing he'd be back,
but you could close your eyes when you were seven

or seventeen and there would be sky. Constellations.
Suns you could name.

Keep your eyes closed. For a few minutes more.
Yes, Nick, I am talking to you.

George Bowering Canadian Parliamentary Poet Laureate

Social Justice

Social without socialism is just a friendly dance
or being polite or something like bees. In school
socials was just their chicken way of saying history
with something added that was never added. Social
eyes are what you wear in your face when you
mingle with intention to make a sale down
the road. Be sociable, our mothers always advised,
when really we were too shy. But didn't we notice,
just about every time the word social came up
it was all about putting on a friendly face? Social
without socialism means finding a strategy to
get ahead, and that means getting more people
behind you, doesn't it? Where's the justice in that?
Just fix your eye on high society, calls for dissociation
from folks that were a lot like you, just us. I've
been up where they prance in slippers, and down
where work boots cost too much, didn't see a lot of
justice either place. Is it around somewhere? The jury's
out on that. Justice without socialism, it's for sale,
isn't it? A jury of your peers has to squint to see
the law and squint again to see whether it's
justifiable in your case. All men and women, some
paper said, are created equal; after that you're
on your own—where's the justice in that? Bees
don't live long but they're always around, until
some operators without socialism kill them while
making money instead of honey. There's a word
for that, and it ain't either of the two up above.

Naomi Long Madgett Poet Laureate of Detroit, Michigan

Dixie Land Blues

Oh, I was born in Dixie, grew up feelin' fear and fright.
Yes, was a boy in Dixie always feelin' dread and fright,
Was scared to leave the safety of Mama's little house at night.

The lynchin's was so frequent couldn't even count 'em all.
Yes, blacks were lynched so often couldn't never count 'em all.
White folks celebrated, laughed and had theirselves a ball.

Well, "Son," my mama tol' me, "we gotta get away from here."
Yes, Mama kept on saying, "Gotta get away from here.
Just can't keep on listenin' to those evil monsters cheer."

One dark moonless midnight, packed some things and slipped away.
Yes, one black cloudy midnight packed our clothes and rode away.
Train would have to get us north before the break of day.

Well, now we're far from Dixie, never will go south no more.
No, never in my lifetime will I go down south no more.
Never felt such freedom, never felt so safe before.

I'm glad I'm not in Dixie. Hooray! Hooray!
In Dixie land I'll never stand 'cause life is hell in Dixie.

127

Crystal Valentine New York City Youth Poet Laureate

I Whip My Hair Back and Forth

The wig itches my scalp like a ringworm
This is my ancestors' punishment for getting too close to a white thing
      The hair is black,

              not blonde

        Brazilian,

           not mine
      I want to be mistaken for a house servant
      Not the master's wife
I want to be sexy
Flex my strong back
      If I bend over I want to be mistaken for a horse

In the club I dance like I'm running from something
My legs pump faster than my heartbeat
      I need this speed to outlive me
          My braids itch beneath my false hair
             My wig cap sways in time with the bass
             The bass assaults the air like the wail of a drum
          And suddenly I am dragged back to feet scraping through
mudded dirt
      I dance like a runaway carriage
I drop it like I'm ducking for cover
I always am

If nothing ever moves,
      Then history will be caught on camera screaming
          Mouth forever frozen in a frightened exhale

          It always finds me in the most joyous of places

I just want to dance like I'm owed something
I just want you to bend me over without pulling off my hair
I slicked down my edges
       I prayed they'd stay in place

We Are Born with Our Hands Bleeding

nails ragged and deformed. After the umbilical cord is cut, doctors examine our calluses to see how long we'll live. A healthy baby has skin so thick, it can't clench its fingers, can't fathom its knuckles around a fist. Mine were eel slick, smooth as water. My parents were told I wouldn't last 2 days.

◆

Childhood is a sick manipulation of time. It was a miracle I'd managed to make it past the age of 7. My birthday was celebrated every 6 months. A heaving double decker cake would be placed in front of me, my knees pressed themselves into the chair cushion just so my head could reach above the table. Rum frosting remained stagnant in the sweltering sway of candle light. I had no child's appetite. I focused on the fire, wondered what kind of bumps and ridges it could conjure upon an undented plane, whether or not it could scorch my palms into a serrated mountain if I provided it with the proper wood.

◆

130

It was 10 years before I could hold a drum. I was no prodigy. My father's talent slid the water off me. He was born a clenched wound, torso wrapped possessively around his *Djembe*. He stretched his mother's placenta tight across the shell's open lip, been banging her rawhide ever since. I'd watch, forgotten, as his open palms skid across the *Djembe's* head, fingertips wrapped and secured—to keep the blood in place—making his drum wail in time with the earth's heartbeat.

Cavana I. O. Faithwalker Poet Laureate of Cleveland Heights, Ohio

Devil's Plague

When the plague is present
others feel the fever
at arm's length they keep you.
There is a stench
it turns their heads downwind.
Watch them lock their car doors
when they feel you walk by.
Women's hands, arms grab
with an
involuntary pinch
at purses as they huddle
and hurry their young.
Men pat pockets
and quicken their steps.
"Those minds are predisposed
to violent thoughts, you know
steal and beat, rape and kill"
they think.
Eyes follow you
and thrust daggers deep
into your flesh. If you
are blessed you are alive
one more day.
From whence comes their contagion
that affects you so deeply
who's to say?

03.18.02

John B. Lee Poet Laureate of Brantford and Norfolk County, Ontario

Beyond the last sandbar

beyond the last sandbar
a small regatta of gulls
float at rest
and they are shell-white
drifting in a barely seeable circle
of windless motion
each gull like a nun's cornette
if a nun were a doll
and the doll were drowned
riding the slow inbreath of resting water
rising and falling to follow old
rhythms of a sleepy measure
in calm dreaming
without foam
where the sky lay fallen
like the lassitude of blue silk settling
drawn on the loom at the hem
by a delicate tugging of a thread-sure hand

and there
to the east
a grey-black armada of Canada geese
wild waterfowl
blinking their webbed feet
coming in and going thence
to groom the beach
with the dropshadow of their reflections
like ash on water
washing away the fire

built overclose to the finality of waves
in the hissing of dampened heat
that flares up and is banked for last burning

overhead
a kettle of vultures
catch thermals
along the black drag of a ragged coast

as a sudden hawk
glides through worried by crows
chased by that caw
going west
to the general rumors of awe

what is it then I wonder
to live in the wind
what is it to be born
in the rough nest
of the aerie
like a storm-broken
orchard
the oriole's pouch
the martin's motel
to thrive in the swamp
or live on the high ledge
overlooking the city

I've seen those chevrons
pulling the dark remainder of day
as it cools
and they're quickening home
to the close at hand shallows
of gloom

it is sweet to remember
and lovely to know
how the forest forgets and the forest recalls
as we enter the earth
like the rain

Rick Kearns Poet Laureate of Harrisburg, Pennsylvania

The Geo-Politics of Uptown Skunks

The enemy of our food
is the fly
so we kill the flies
that used to fill the webs
of the 6 spider species
co-habitating with us
in our vintage duplex
uptown
and now the spiders need
other things to eat
so they fill every empty
space in and around my house
in search of other sustenance.
Can't walk out the backdoor
without ducking to the right
in order to avoid a mouth full
of gossamer goodness.

The enemies of the spreading suburbs
are the trees and animals that make
it impossible to lay block to
build foundations that do not include
homes for skunks and opossum
so the skunks hang in
my backyard and rumble with
alley cats and other varmints
hunting at night
shooting defensive stink clouds
which rise majestically
and seep through the old windows

of my dear old house
while I'm watching TV.

The enemies of the Russians
way back when
were the Taliban fighters
amassing in Afghanistan so we
gave them missiles and rifles and cash.
And one of those mujahideen
was a guy named Osama Bin Laden
who hated Saddam Hussein
whose family was friends with
our friends in Saudi Arabia
and the enemy of our enemy was
who now?
The enemy of our enemy is
whose friend?

I think that now
I am an enemy to
the enemy-of-our-enemy
is-our-friend theory.
With friends like Baby Doc
Somoza and Pinochet
I think it's time
we just focus on
making friends with people
who don't want to kill
their own people
or us
or the spiders
or the skunks.

I choose peace
please.

Joyce Sutphen Minnesota Poet Laureate

Eleanor Beardsley in Paris

"There are no newspapers in Paris today"
she reports—"all part of an ongoing
dispute between labor groups and the French
government over President François
Hollande's plan to overhaul the country's
labor policies." She says this in a voice
that has gone from English to French,
from one set of vowels to another, as if
she is our French cousin intoning the words
in a flat bemused way that could only
come from having spent ages waiting
in line at the boulangerie; she says these
things in the weary voice of someone
who has covered elections, riots, student
demonstrations, the Tour de France,
and terrorist attacks in Paris and Brussels;
she says these things in the voice of
someone who loves how all the windows
in Paris open up in the summer so that
the sound of plates and silverware blends
with the sound of someone playing the
piano or laughing, and a gypsy jazz band
gathers under the window one night
and everyone throws silver coins down
into the narrow cobblestone street.

Rita Dove United States Poet Laureate (born in Akron, Ohio)

Lady Freedom Among Us

don't lower your eyes
or stare straight ahead to where
you think you ought to be going

don't worry *oh no*
not another one
get a job   fly a kite
go bury a bone

with her oldfashioned sandals
with her leaden skirts
with her stained cheeks and whiskers and heaped up trinkets
she has risen among us in blunt reproach

she has fitted her hair under a hand-me-down cap
and spruced it up with feathers and stars
slung over one shoulder she bears
the rainbowed layers of charity and murmurs
all of you   even the least of you

don't cross to the other side of the square
don't think *another item to fit on a tourist's agenda*

consider her drenched gaze   her shining brow
she who has brought mercy back into the streets
and will not retire politely to the potter's field

having assumed the thick skin of this town
its gritted exhaust its sunscorch and blear

she rests in her weathered plumage
bigboned   resolute

don't think you can ever forget her
don't even try
she's not going to budge

no choice but to grant her space
crown her with sky
for she is one of the many
and she is each of us

Joel Lipman Poet Laureate of Lucas County, Ohio

make them think I am king

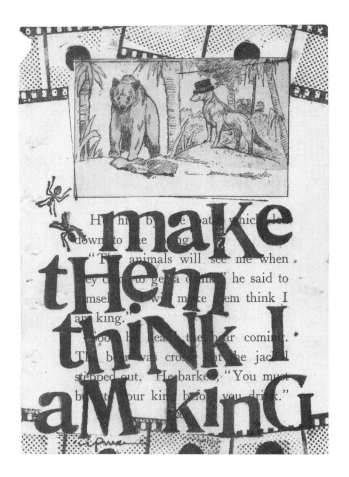

SPEAK UP

"Hate must be exposed and denounced . . . An informed and unified community is the best defense against hate."

Jim Ferris Poet Laureate of Lucas County, Ontario

Comprehensive List
of All Benefits
to Being Disabled
in Contemporary America

1. Sometimes u get
   ♿ood parkin♿.

2. If u want someone
   to pray 4 u,
   someone will. At length.

3. If u want
   someone
   to agree yr
   better off
   DEAD
   some1
   will. = rights.

4. The lowest of expectations.
   Good boy. Now shake hands. Beg.

5. Sometimes people will
   hold the door 4 u.
   Even if u don't want
   2 go in.

6. See #1

Rebecca Zseder Mississauga Youth Poet Laureate, Ontario

Voices

I've been told to brush my hair 100 strokes a section before bed.
Preventing knots prevents breakage, or at least protects against it.
Keeps it smooth, pretty, healthy, pretty, soft . . .
Keeps you aware of how close you are to fragility.
Keeps you in front of a mirror
Reminded of how much of you is show and tell.
Smooth. Pretty. Healthy. Pretty. Soft . . .
I've been told which parts of my face need painting before presentation.
Highlighting your features helps more than harms.
Keep this light, this dark, this big, and this covered
Remind yourself every morning that your face fades too quickly to be out there alone.
Remind yourself always that even your skin isn't good enough.
Stay in front of that mirror.
So much of you is show and tell.
I have opened history books of male domination, baffled at how rarely women seemingly spoke.
Wondering how easy it must be to steal a voice and get away with it when the thief only ever stood in front of a microphone.
Wondering how loud I have to speak to be heard through that glass ceiling.
Wondering if the glass is as fragile as those who built it must be.
If there is something shameful in hiding a voice, what can be said about muting an entire gender.
I say, speak up.
Brush your hair 100 times to improve your arm strength.
Remind yourself that persistence makes perfection possible.
Keep yourself aware of how close you are to fragility, keep yourself aware that the once weak are always the most strong.

Paint your face before presentation, with the war paint of those who fought before you.

Remind them that you are far more than enough.

Remind them that the only colour added will be the shade of your blood running red with courage.

Remind them that your skin is better than armour.

Shatter the ceiling with the shrieks of the lost women, of the women who tried, of the women who spoke and were shunned, of the women who spoke and were shot, of the women who spoke and were quoted by a man later mentioned in that history book.

Write your own story; write your own relevance; make them all watch you rise.

My favourite part of looking in a mirror has always been the background.

It reminds me of how I can see beyond myself.

Keeps me aware of how much time women have been given to watch and to plan.

Mirrors can be shattered with the fragility of glass.

It is time for show and tell, I bare my skin, my hair, my soft and my pretty.

I use war paint and my history book to remind me why I fight.

I don't remind myself that I am strong for a girl.

I remind myself that I am strong.

I don't use a microphone because women never needed help to speak.

My voice is amplified by the shadows of voices who once came before me.

We are the voices now.

The voices of the women unmuted, uncensored, un-stolen.

The voices of the women who always knew how to speak.

I've been told to brush my hair 100 strokes a section before bed.

I tell them, I don't take well to being told what to do.

Christine Howey Poet Laureate of Cleveland Heights, Ohio

I Was a Male Impersonator for 40 Years

No, not like a drag king, that kind of thing No highness for the lowness I was feeling. See, I was born in 1945, four month after FDR died . . . 2 days after the end of World War II . . . 20 years before the invention of Doritos. We're talking a long, long, looong time ago.

So everybody's happy back then, and so am I. I mean, the first five years I'm down with it all: Drooling, learning how to walk and talk and crap into a porcelain chair. Hey, I got this! Then . . . BOOM: I'm five years old in 1950. Kindergarten! "Boys here, girls there." Whoa! Say what?? Boys? Girls? When did we get divided into teams? And why wasn't I consulted about this? And I'm on WHAT team? The BOY team?

Hang on, hold up, we gotta talk about this but nobody's talking, they just shove me into stiff blue jeans, hand me a Roy Rogers rifle and say, "Be a man, little man!" Be a man . . . be a man . . . how can I be a man when I don't know how to be a person yet? Hey, I just got done figuring out peek-a-boo and now I gotta be a little man because I got this thing down here? Because of this? Seriously? This thing is way less than one percent of my total body weight and IT'S gonna determine how I live my life? Seriously? Seriously???

Oh yeah, they're serious, I can see that and I know if I tell them I'm a really a girl it's gonna go bad for me . . . see, this is the early fifties and they weren't fuckin' around with gender and shit. There was no: "Oh, you have a gender identity problem? Please, tell us!" It was: "You be who we tell you are or you're in deep trouble, little man, this is going on your permanent record. And if you don't come around we'll hook some jumper cables up to your skull and run a few thousand Reddy Kilowatts from your frontal lobe down to your brainstem until we fry us up a nice, calm, obedient boy."

So I shut the fuck up and hide inside my plaid short sleeve shirts as I click off the mile markers: Boom: Ten years old, I'm a boy who doesn't talk much because I'm afraid of making a mistake and letting people see who I really am. Boom: 20 years old, I'm a young man, drinking hard and protesting Vietnam. Boom: 30 years old, I'm a married man with a child. Boom: 40 years old, I'm an advertising executive man with a red sports car and I'm suicidal because the girl, the woman inside me is dying, I feel her dying, she's been waiting for 40 years and now she's dying. And my male impersonator act is dying and I'm dying way before my time.

And then . . . Boom: I'm 45 in 1990 and I say that's all. I won't die in rented room wearing borrowed clothes. I won't be what you want and I won't bleed for what you need . . . you cannot supersede me or impede me because I am no longer weak-kneed. So you can speed-read the end of this screed: I am Christine. I am . . . Christine.

Christine Howey Poet Laureate of Cleveland Heights, Ohio

The Female Circumspection Act

My fellow Americans and faithful promise keepers, I address you this evening not just as your Pastor/Vice-President, but also as your trusted advisor on the path towards true religious liberty.

As you know, last year our recent passage of the Limbaugh "Slut Stopper" Amendment, enabling male employers to determine the specific health care needs of their female employees while simultaneously criminalizing contraception, was a divine step in the direction of gospel-girded, Jesus-bedazzled freedom.

Empowered by that success, we are moving forward with legislation that we are calling the Female Circumspection Act. As you know, my lambs of righteousness and virtue, wayward females tend not to observe the value of circumspection, those maidenly impulses of modesty that should lead virginal creatures to be cautious and careful at every moment of every day.

No, we have found that most contemporary women are ruled by the twin devils of genital mania common to their hysterical gender: clitoral convulsions and labial delirium. As a result, since women lack the good sense and solid decision-making that men receive from their orgasmic organs—those rock hard rods of truth, those staffs tumescent with calm rationality—women must be protected from their own spasmodic and unhinged natural state by a benevolent government.

To those who sneer that we are not treating women as people, I say nonsense. In fact, not only are women people, they are much more than people. They are the instruments of our survival as a species, and the government has a right—nay, a duty—to husband those female reproductive systems just as we would seek to protect a vital industrial plant or a pure water reservoir.

The Female Circumspection Act has been demeaned by its opponents as nothing more than a Female Circumcision Act, but nothing could be further from the truth. The Act simply requires that pre-pubescent girls be relieved of the demon-drenched body parts of perversity that Satan affixed to their bodies, no doubt when God was not watching.

By excising the clitoris and labia (minora and majora), females will be freed from the chains of their oppressive sex and be able to stand beside, and slightly to the rear of, their male mentors and guides. With female sexual satisfaction no longer an issue, marriages will become contentedly male-centered, men will be freed from the high-pitched carping and criticism that lead to performance anxiety, and peace will overtake our crusading patriarchal culture.

Good day, and a-men.

Craig Czury Poet Laureate of Berks County, Pennsylvania

Let The Poets In

The ship is sunk and the damage is done
someone
let the poets in
Let the poets in on the glass slashed
basketball courts in the city parks
The ship is sunk
with its head of steam trains
smoking through the abandoned shopping outlet
plywood spray painted windows
The damage is all
let the poets in on the graffiti laced
basement walls of the YMCA church camp
The Olivets pool table green velvet
sliced up its belly with the long stiletto stroke
of a stick on cue
Let the needle-breath misfit poets in
where they belong homeless at the shelter
Shuffling the hair-stench paper hallways
of the State Hospital
with their i.v. pens looking for the key
Staring into their home cooked rice & gandules
at the Puerto Rican Latin Association
while listening to the broken whip lash
triple tongue gun fire staccato echo off the pagoda
Let the poets in after school
after a lifetime
flunking school to do their homework
in the darkly lit corners of the Police Athletic League
Let the poets in

to weave their elbow spider web rhythmic flashlights
in the neo-blindered eyes of Boyertown
In the neo-kindred eyes of this new kind of city pay-off
Yes
from under the rubble
from under the vials and casings
through the debris of gaping cracks
out of the bowed heads silent over a sheet of paper
as if in prayer
Reading
turn on your lights the cockroaches will scatter
Let the poets
In the beginning in
by saying

Pauletta Hansel Poet Laureate of Cincinnati, Ohio

Passage

I was fourteen;
they were older.
I was trying hard
to fill the woman's body
that I occupied—its breasts
and monthly bleeding—the way
later I'd fill rented rooms
with thrift store furniture.
Nothing ever matched.
Mostly I learned the female art
of silence. To hold my tongue
against my teeth,
my questions veiled
by downturned eyes.
It was easier to pass
for grown with men.
Women wanted to spread
wings to take me under
or to nudge me
from their perches—
no room for three.
Men wanted only
hands against the parts
of me that grew up first.
They were older.
I was fourteen.

Written in response to a line in "Bike Ride
with Older Boys" by Laura Kasischke.

Anna Yin Poet Laureate of Mississauga, Ontario

Thirteen Ways of Looking at Smog

—after Wallace Stevens

I

mountains or bridges?
cannot tell . . .
we are only the moving blackbirds

II

Blue sky—merely a dream,
green—out of sight,
black somber escorts . . .

III

in this dark watercolor
under a red alarm
we fantasize feathers pure

IV

plunging, plunging,
nearly all indexes . . .
except the Air Quality

V

speechless,
masks against tongues . . .
newspaper's brazen statement: non-toxic

VI

blue skies shy away
dark nights . . .
darkened eyes

VII

Ignorance is Strength . . .
today's hotline:
crimes for wearing masks!

VIII

$2 + 2 = 5$ . . .
in dreams,
someone is coughing

IX

watch out!
watch in
and out . . .

X

out of order!
who fashions
this tide of smog disaster . . .

XI

poison thick in the air
poison sinks into the body
poison leadens our wings . . .

XII

mountains or bridges?
it doesn't matter . . .
we are blackbirds still

XIII

in this dark watercolor
at the dark dawn
we lose our feathers

George Kalamaras Indiana Poet Laureate

For All the Russian Wolfhounds—the Borzoi— Slaughtered During the Revolution, 1917

They killed you, dear ones,
because of wealth. Not wealth, really,
but excess. You were noble by birth,
called *borzój*, meaning *swift*. Princes
kept you like fast-moving paintings
to elegant their rooms. Palaces perfected you.
All that sighthound blood imported from Arabia,
crossed with Tartar coursing hounds, and you were suddenly
as delicate and fleeting as a Monet lily.
If the St. Petersburg ballet whirled into my heart,
where you now rest, fireside, snoozing
on a rug, you would strengthen the troupe
with your powerful frame, deep chest,
and slightly arched loin. Who but you
could chase, catch, and hold its quarry?—mostly
wolves driven from the forest into the open field
where huntsmen of czars and one hundred or more of you
waited. It was not your fault that the wealthy
loved you. You were not just beautiful but there to quiet howling
bad dreams in blowing midnight snow. Your mostly white fur
blanching our fear of the dark. It was you
who rewrote the tales, who barked
three times and freed the woodcutter from Stepnaya
from the spell of his tree-root
tree sorrow. From his axe and saw. You who,
disguised as a prince, traveled to Yuriatin and the Urals
and kissed the woman back into her body
from an owl-wing concoction of sleep. Lenin and Trotsky

hated you, saw in your long legs the lengthening
hoards of beggars, soup lines, and winter trash in barrels
burning the street. The offerings of typhoid, boils, and flu
raked endlessly through snow. But you licked the hand of all men
equally, would curl at the feet—if you could—of the most ragged
woman, her woolen cloak torn and soot-filled. Had it not been
for the English importing some of your forebears
forty years sooner, your death would have no descendent.
Your expression was a persistent smile, mouth open
and drawn back, as if—even when still—you were constantly running
headlong into wooded winds, or calmly rejecting a disposition of sad.
Like I am sad, by the fire, this crisp November night,
ninety-nine years late to save you, to calm
your cries and blood and dark throaty
notes. Ninety-nine years to say the Bolsheviks
rightly believed in sharing roof and bread,
but the Revolution and killing should not
have included innocent you. Or fifty-one years late,
to say—after first seeing *Dr. Zhivago* (and maybe thirty times since)—
I still hear murmuring words *not* said in the film,
but buried there, all this time, in a vastness
of ground fog and deepening snow. There,
sorrowing my throat, as I struggle to say: *I'm so sorry.*
I'm so sorry. I'm so sorry. I'm so sorry.

George Kalamaras Indiana Poet Laureate

Pack-A-Day Dog

> Based on a photo of a beagle, one of the pack-a-day smoking dogs at the
> laboratory at the Hanford Atomic Plant, pictured with Gilbert Brown, supervisor
> of a colony of 200 beagles used in various experiments, and
> Dr. J. F. Park, senior research scientist, 1966

Pack-A-Day Dog?
So much depends
upon a

name. Glazed in pain
water, halfway down
the throat-scar

throat. What pricks! Anyone knows
I try to limit
swearing to *snail poop*

and *eel-scum, belly-button
lint* and *sparrow droppings
in the sink*, though I slip at

times, like mud hens in
rain. But these men, their science
man eyes. What if we

observed, measured,
meted them out, moving *them*
in and out of the

cage? What if the
experiment was *sensitivity*,
and we named *them*,

Sea-lice in the ear
or *Rusty nail through
the sole of the*

foot? So much, so
little, depends upon
screaming at them

eel-lint! or *belly-button
scum!* Anyone knows
I try to forgive

most anyone, any
thing. Not these men.
Not this time.

Roger Nash Poet Laureate of Sudbury, Ontario

The Shell-Shocked Rocking Chair

He came back from undeclared wars
of "international aid," and rocked
in his rocking chair for five—
ten—twenty—years,
seldom talking to his wife,
or even his fully understanding,
but equally untalkative, cat.

Silent as the mildewed wrists
of machine-gunned teenagers:
soldiers, who lied—but for the honesty
of their cause—about age, then abruptly
fell through their deaths, which, like adolescent
dreams, were entirely beyond
any words they had time to find.

The remembered drum of guns,
his wife's rhythmic cloth
on his brow, unite in one
contradictory thing: a far-flung
polyphony, both loud and soft,
of rustling maps of points
of attack and train timetables

—to grandmother's tea-parties.
One music can be heard,
but only with lips tight shut.
Otherwise, to say "This is this,"

"That is that," sunders
"This!"—the guns—to boom
entirely, and accurately, on their own.

Rather, keep teeth bolted
under shrink-wrapped lips.

Anna Yin Poet Laureate of Mississauga, Ontario

Dance of the Old Year, 2016

The last day of the year
the dance lady called for help—
all the passing days of tragedies
piling with Leonard Cohen's
"You want it darker"

into the dark. It was
silence, her silence
when we fetched her,
no more the pretty woman
but a ragged bag-lady.

The city in its birthday mood
dressed up for party after party—
dancing, gambling, fooling
with plenty of alcohol, balloons,
chocolate, slogans and thrills.

Yet in the dark, leaves
fell like lost souls,
each peeling down
from the old year's calendar,

the silly winds picking them up
then reassembling them
into a hollow man
who fiercely danced his dream.

Patricia Clark Poet Laureate of Grand Rapids, Michigan

West of Syria

They washed up on a beach, the small
                    bodies of children—
        a little boy of just three years.
                    It was not the sea's fault.

It was not the fault of the rubber raft.
                    We do not have life jackets so small,
        the smugglers said. It will be brief,
                    the crossing to Italy, they added.

The gendarme takes a photo, then picks up
                    the boy's body—wearing shorts, a bright
                        summer top, and sandals. Once,
        there was a future, smiles, laughter,
                    once he had a brother and mother.

They drowned in the same sea. It was not
                    a blessing that the father lived.
        The mother was twenty-seven years old.
                    What they wanted was a better life.
To want is to risk, and to take a chance
                    is how a risk is made tangible.

    Into the smugglers' hands, crumpled bills.
When the rubber raft came,
                    the father objected. Will we be safe?

The boy washed up on a beach, the waves
                    lapping against his still mouth,
                        as though he were sleeping,
as though you could make a pillow of sand.

Otter Jung-Allen Philadelphia Youth Poet Laureate

The Man on the Train *or,*
What I Have Been Named Into

I held your hand on the train.
the man leaning against the doors
must have thought this was his summons.
he stared at us with a blunt, edgeless hatred.
his lip raised against his teeth.
he spit without moving.
I felt the wind dug from me,
and the places of us separated.
if he had spoken or pushed us,
I would not have flinched so hard.
he had done what he had set out to do that morning.
he had put on a hat, brushed his teeth,
and left the house doing what he called God's work.
how big of him, I thought,
to think God couldn't handle
His own to do list.
and how many people did he retrieve from heaven
on the train home,
and call it what God
would have wanted?

Christine Howey Poet Laureate of Cleveland Heights, Ohio

I'm Gonna Get the DTs over DT in the DC

I'm gonna get the DTs over DT in the DC
because I haven't stopped drinking since
he won the election
and maybe you think I'm drowning my sorrows
or then again maybe you think I'm celebrating
but either way this isn't a good position to be in
because I'm gonna get the DTs over DT in the DC
wondering if he knows about the Nuclear Triad
which I'm guessing he thinks are hot blonde triplets
with toothy smiles and huge racks who want to have
their cats grabbed by the Commander in Chief
Holy fuck, Donald Trump is the Commander in Chief . . .
I'll have another drink, make it a double,
and I'm gonna get the DTs over DT in the DC
because I think if he tweets an insult to China
deep in the night when I'm asleep
and they take it seriously,
because they take *everything* seriously,
and they launch nuclear missiles, one of them may
land on my porch and pretty much ruin
my fucking day
so I'm gonna get the DTs over DT in the DC—
hey, I need a martini, who has a fucking vodka martini????
because he may want to abolish Social Security
because why not? and yes,
I'm old and I paid into Social Security for 48 years, and
counting, and if he leaves me out
I'm gonna need martinis delivered to my house every
hour on the hour and that's why

I'm gonna get the DTs over DT in the DC
so you'll probably see me on the street, wandering around
like I don't know where I am because DT's in the DC
and I'm trapped in some motherfucking navel-lint-picking,
sweaty-Cleveland-Browns-knit-hat-wearing
cartoonist's goddamn graphic fantasy novel in which DT
gets elected president and takes my liver hostage!
That's why I'm gonna get the DTs over DT in the DC!

Marvin Bell Iowa Poet Laureate (born in New York, New York)

Little Napoleon
or: Foreign Policy

Our little Napoleon is bigger than your little Napoleon.

Heather H. Thomas Poet Laureate of Berks County, Pennsylvania

Atonement

after Barnett Newman

Which one travels
toward the stranger?

Who in nightspeed slits
of borders, time zones

word-maps crossing
multilingual

what's on the tongue
risking trust

without translation
atonement in a zip of light

drawn across the sky's
at(one)ment

as the light shifts
but does not separate

one with other, one.

Pauletta Hansel Poet Laureate of Cincinnati, Ohio

November 10, 2016

Today in Orange County, Florida,
a bald eagle got trapped
in a storm drain.
What I know about
Florida or eagles
could fit on the tip of this pen
(and never would I have thought
them together on the page)
but I do know something
about metaphor when it
wings up to flap in my face
and that something is flailing
flightless, with talons,
on the breath of a country—
mine—
suspended.
I am waiting
for the worst that can happen.
I'm afraid
we've seen nothing yet.

Joel Lipman Poet Laureate of Lucas County, Ohio

HOW MA / NY FLAGS / WERE TOO / MANY FLA / GS FOR / THE DEAD

LOBBY LEADERS

"Elected officials and other community leaders can be important allies [in the fight against hate]."

Right now, take the time to write a letter about the social justice issues you truly care about and send it to:

The President of the United States
The White House
1600 Pennsylvania Avenue NW
Washington, DC 20500

Write now. Let your voice be heard.

Rita Dove United States Poet Laureate (born in Akron, Ohio)

Freedom Ride

As if, after High Street
and the left turn onto Exchange
the view would veer onto
someplace fresh: Curaçao,
or a mosque adrift on a milk-fed pond.
But there's just more cloud cover,
and germy air
condensing on the tinted glass,
and the little houses with
their fearful patches of yard
rushing into the flames.

Pull the cord a stop too soon, and
you'll find yourself walking
a gauntlet of stares.
Daydream, and you'll wake up
in the stale dark of a cinema,
Dallas playing its mistake over and over
until even that sad reel won't stay
stuck—there's still
Bobby and Malcolm and Memphis,
at every corner the same
scorched brick, darkened windows.

Make no mistake: There's fire
back where you came from, too.
Pick any stop: You can ride
into the afternoon singing with strangers,

or rush home to the scotch
you've been pouring all day—
but where you sit is where you'll be
when the fire hits.

Marvin Bell Iowa Poet Laureate (born in New York, New York)

The Book of the Dead Man (Desperate in America)

> Live as if you were already dead.
>
> —Zen admonition

1. About the Dead Man Desperate in America

The dead man can't stop to sleep.

The daily news lingers late into the nights.

He sees men robbing banks with toy guns.

He sees the impoverished and sickly banging on the prison doors.

The president and his party don't care, they have health insurance that
    includes cuticle control.

They have pensions built from gouging the planet.

They eat oil and coal and stay out of the sun.

They fly the flag of rampant capitalism, the pennants of death to the poor.

2. More About the Dead Man Desperate in America

The perfume they import cannot make them smell better.

They are the privileged in private towers, the idolaters of gold leaf.

They smell of steak sauce and potions taken from people of color who
    hoped to survive.

They make medicine unaffordable.

The dead man hears the creak among the cogs, the slippage of the belt, the
    chugging of the racists and anti-Semites laboring uphill.

Let their time be short, their hollow chests sputter and their teeth fall out,
    for they are the party of death.

A president befitting a mob, a First Family that cares only for itself.
The party in power a-twitter while the opposition has covered the mirrors.

March 25, 2017

Andrea Scarpino Poet Laureate of the Upper Peninsula, Michigan

There Was a Man [excerpts]

There was a man.
We were friends, so many years.
Me, him, his wife.
So many nights I spent at their house.
So many coffee shops, so many visits
after I moved away.
We wrote and wrote, sent articles we liked,
funny stories, poems about parents dying
(my father, dead. Then their fathers, dead.)
His wife called me *Dearest*,
signed her cards with Xs and Os.
We talked fashion,
Alexander McQueen, Italian jeans,
shoes too beautiful to wear.
We talked about our dogs.
We talked writing, ballet,
LA traffic, what we were reading.
When I bought a house, they sent a set of knives.
When they retired, they sent a box of purses
nicer than I could afford. So many letters
for so many holidays.
We were friends, I mean to say. I mean
to tell myself: we were friends
and we did friend-things.

◆

We were at a conference. Him, his wife, me.
We ate together, night after night,
sat together during readings.
When I was alone, one asked me

to join them, asked about my day.
We were at a cocktail hour, not late
but it was dark outside, raining.
People sat on couches, stood in tight circles,
held napkins and plastic cups
with shards of ice. The heat, humidity.
I stood with a woman whose eyes were so blue
I felt I'd never look away.
And then someone was touching me.
A man. My friend. In a room
where people stood laughing, talking.
His hand on me. And he walked away.
Did he just touch you? Her eyes so beautiful
I could not lie. The man, my friend,
sat on a couch facing us, stirred his drink, stared
our way. We kept talking. He stood again,
joined us. *Aren't you going to say something?*
he asked. I looked at him. *What should I say?*
We were at a conference with writers,
editors, agents, people who publish books
and magazines. The room steamed
with rain, humidity, with conversation.
His wife in another room, talking, laughing.
I could see her through the doorway,

her hands, moving.
The woman with blue eyes.
I could not lie to her but I told no one else.
Next day at lunch, a man I didn't know
asked me if I had heard the gossip—
Word on the street—and then he spoke
out loud what had happened to me.

◆

There was a man. A president.
A man who wanted to be president—

At least 24 women have accused
the Republican presidential nominee
of inappropriate sexual behavior
in multiple incidents spanning
the last 30 years—including groping
and kissing them without permission—
I've gotta use some Tic Tacs
just in case I start kissing her. You know
I'm automatically attracted to beautiful—
I just start kissing them. It's like a magnet.
Just kiss. I don't even wait.
And when you're a star they let you do it.
You can do anything.
Grab them by the pussy.
You can do anything—
A man who wanted to be president and was—
You have to treat 'em like shit—

Fred Wah Canadian Parliamentary Poet Laureate

Re Politics of Location

Locate the texture, streets, ravines, wolf-
willow, names for grasses, that space of field
between the barn and the forest, edges
in performance, such as putting your hand in
or putting a handle on the local magazine
chip in since writing's *locus solus* isn't
history's place anyplace . . . and get lost
please forward "From in Here . . ." 1976
or Great Lakes blackout 1964, Place,
as the Montana lady said, is what you have left
my own Kootenay River, then rivers north
of Waiting for Saskatchewan, Loki's still buried
at Smoky Creek, even beyond the Ontario orchard
spreads out *viz* who you are is where
you are Earth further studies location's
navigation to make political Miss Edge in
Nation no noun in that *sitkum* today
quick hammering of the jake brakes
on the outskirts where
was never the problem animal is, still
there "breathin' it with a sigh"

Siduri Beckman Philadelphia Youth Poet Laureate

Women's March

I'm taking this kernel
    And swallowing it to keep it
        In the pit of my stomach
It's encrusted with gunk of our nation but I'll shine it
          Down with acidic
    Words I keep in my gut
        Bearing the brunt of all those
        Nights and dawns you spent fighting
While I kept sleeping.
I know what lies behind I can read but
    I will never know unless I take
    The stones in my shoes and put them
    Next to yours so that we might
        Run this last part

    Barefoot.

Joel Lipman Poet Laureate of Lucas County, Ohio

George Popham

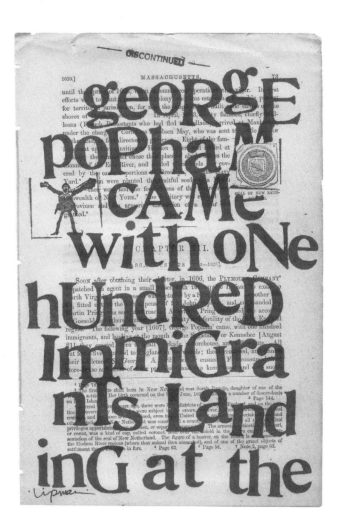

LOOK
LONG RANGE

"Expand your community's comfort zones
so you can learn and live together."

Wendy Vardaman Poet Laureate of Madison, Wisconsin

@ChazenArtUW at the *First Folio Exhibit* the day after a woman loses the presidency like a heart balloon ripped from her fist

> For the master's tools will never dismantle the master's house. They may allow us temporarily to beat him at his own game, but they will never enable us to bring about genuine change. And this fact is only threatening to those women who still define the master's house as their only source of support.
>
> —Audre Lorde

> My lord, as I was sewing in my closet . . .
> —Ophelia to Polonius

my mother twisted coat hanger into shape then basted
a ruffled ring of stiff net to its wire. insisted
on making a valentines' box I might or might not have made
myself after she got home from work. my dad may or may
not have been reciting Hamlet lines to a mirror
at his elbow. my brother most certainly watching tv.

my lord as I was sewing in my closet, measuring wire to thread
the needle of your need, feeling sew so, knot knowing what you felt.
knot knowing who/what. my ayes began to go. knot sew sharp as they
    were wants.
missing the whole. missing you. dropping stitch after stitch.
turning the hoop. looping together what split in two.
tough muscle so hard to pierce. to draw twist through.

writing your name in blood on skin.
words. words. words. words. words.

187

⬧　⬧　⬧

maybe O sews her own heart
back together in the closet. maybe Gertrude
shows her how some afternoon. *cross-stitch with care—*
back/forth down/up over/through
no need to look. so
many tasks that women do seam
like that. the hand keeps an eye on somebody
while the ear watches someone

who doesn't watch back. you don't connect with other
people. *back. forth.* you never have. *down.*
up. this is an overdue valentine
for my mother. *over.*
through. whose Wards store placed clothing orders for Hillary
in Arkansas c. 1972. *back. forth.* who didn't connect to you.

⬧　⬧　⬧

while I pried my father's hands off aluminum cans & glass more than won
knight to send him to sleep. know matter. my mother still made the
　　valentines' box
with a ruffle-wired heart, *Hamlet* scratched across her chest—

to be or not to be twisted like copper around & through
tissue & artery to hold it there. & scratch again when it disappeared.
Hamlet. we wrote. & wrote. & wrote. & wrote

we've been chipping against his shine with pens & needles
when glass can be spun. woven. knit. crimped. bent.

wake up, sweet ladies. Hamlet's cracked mirror is not for you.

yours knot for hem.

if I have to cut you out of my art, then mend
it once an hour, I will. if I have to make this the last word I type

& poem in sewn paper. in rick rack & button. in wrinkle
& torn. in silkscreen & pressure. in saddle stitch & barbed wire net

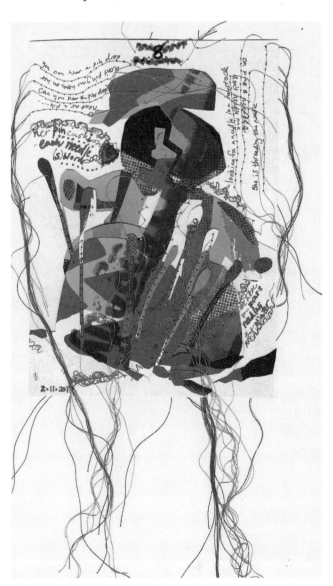

Kimberly Blaeser Wisconsin Poet Laureate

Tribal Mound, Earth Sutra

> Our wealth abounds
>
> within what we preserve.
>
> —Allison Adelle Hedge Coke, *Blood Run*

We remain
wealthy beyond measure,
the past—ancient treasure we protect.

What power resides in earthen mounds?
Ancestors, wisdom of clan relatives,
astrological continuities, portal to spiritual realities.

Effigy of bird, panther, rabbit, bear
the hungry rise of earth imbued with sacred life,
monument, transcendent force.
Name this site—holy.

Stand with me here
a fragile human thread, earth sutra.
This curved land an ageless link
we a small vibration
one song among the many.

Sing this song now.
My heritage, yours.
Shape in consecrated breath
words that mean: belong

honor, courage, praise, believe . . .
protect.
Transform with me here,
become in this sanctuary
rich in memory,
humble before mystery.
Open the medicine pouch
of your voice,
stand firm together
defend this treasure.
Yes, we remain.

Tom Cull Poet Laureate of London, Ontario

After Rivers

—after City Parks (2016, photograph on paper),
by Nicholas Cote

i

I've waded below the Hunt Weir
where the dam drops the river
into vortices of water
pinning drunken swimmers
by their shoulders to the bottom.

Low-head dam, drowning machines
they're called, but the fishing's good—
I've been pulled by swirling eddies
an 18-foot pole in hand, fashioned
from pipes bought at home depot
a fishing net bolted to one end.

In august the water is low
I net plastic bottles, cans,
tim hortons cups,
a flip-flop, diaper, needles
caught in the elliptical froth.
Anglers eye me cautiously—
one pulls a carp from the depths,
its carnival colours like a backyard koi;
I catch a neon pink stuffy

snagged on a branch
and toss it back on shore.

ii

The river transports   Ce n'est pas une rivière
to the Pacific   outside it slithers by, beyond the gallery glass,
our dollar store pottage,   past the workers rebuilding the London Dyke.
we'll live there soon—   But the waters will have their way—
fog catchers,   they will again break these banks,
salted, dried, and hung—   drown us in our beds, carry our bodies
building our empire   aloft downstream, jostled like bloated
on the flotsam, jetsam   frat boys in blow up sumo suits.
filtered by rivers.   This is the dawning of the age of aquariums.

iii

What does the river convey?
It is hard to say:
wood, cement, grain
rice, chair, ink jet
copic markers, water colours
crayon, rag and paper,
acrylic, charcoal, faux fur stuffing,
glass beads, duct-tape—

Printed on
etched on
cut out
glazed
your brush will paint blue-green algae
on the canvas of a perch's belly.

It is hard to say:
Askunessippi, Antler River,
La Tranche, The Thames
Deshkan Ziibi

all the tangled narratives
in the abandoned place.

Dennis Hinrichsen Lansing Poet Laureate

[short film with gun and flame]

Earl Little's home, 1929, Lansing

—and so they watched the fire burn / these brave
men with water /

the flames reflected in the balls
of their eyes

because that's what cinema does
—it frames / it provides the close-up

—this second
fire

which is just their hatred on a slow hiss /
house like a whole

hill of crosses burning /
the Lord

in it / *their* Lord / first klansmen /
evident only

in bleeding sap / ark of a family
hustling down evening's scarred waterline

—to where / *cut* /
—for safety? /

cut / moon high in a tree / bone-limbed /
cut / like a piece of fire

on fire / dead stars / woman out
on a lawn / child

at her hip / face
half-buried in the billowing skirt

—eye
embered / mind

spangled /
numb / *cut* //

fast forward / 4th
of July //

I have to move my car to protect it
from my neighbors' rockets

—two hours of constant shelling / here /
blocks away / the desire

to blow things up so pure
it does not have to stop to reload

—an aneurysm in perpetuity /
strontium for blood /

copper for sky /
gold for iron / because that's what it took then /

takes / now /
for *white*

—pig iron will to sanction such a hurt
—*montage* / exploding night / my

car's re-parked
soundtrack / grind of traffic down MLK

to Malcolm X
—and then that straight shot to the interstate

—windshields greased with breath and
hurry /

hatred / rages / passion / lies
—child

of a child
of man who might have watched /

or set the match / barreling east
—each small town /

all the way to Howell /
a garden

of blossom and
flame / up-

turned faces
—*awed eyes*—awash in this night's glory / *cut* /

—Earl Little running / with a gun / as if to murder the sky

Samuel Hazo Pennsylvania Poet Laureate

Signs of Life in a Sundown City

We number less than half of what
　　we were four decades back.
The young look elsewhere for their lives.
The old grow older and die.
Mansions of a long dead gentry
　　calcify like skulls.
　　　　　　　　　　Museums
lease from millionaires what artists
painted while they starved.
　　　　　　　　　　　　On streets
that once were prime, the smell
of oligarchy gone bourgeois is palpable.
The current synonym for blackjack,
　　poker, craps and slots
　　is gaming.
　　　　　　　　Uptown at midnight
the currency is drugs and guns,
and murderers grow younger
by the day.
　　　　　　　Regardless, the trees
parade in place at permanent
attention.
　　　　　　Simply by happening,
each day proclaims itself unique
and unrepeatable.
　　　　　　　　And two
undaunted rivers fork and fuse
into a third that flows into a fourth
that steers in silence to the sea
that's stayed the same since Genesis.

Sue MacLeod Poet Laureate of Halifax, Nova Scotia (born in Kingston, Ontario)

It's okay if we wreck this planet

The technology will exist by then
to airlift us all
to another

Saucers   hovering

like judgmentday.com but—

collecting
everyone:

the meek
the halt
the dispossessed
the youth-at-risk

departing: Livernois & Joy
                      departing: Jane & Finch

the legions

lifted
one by one

onto the radiant

apparatus

head lamps pulsing

through the barrio   the sinking

archipelago

the secret   & not
labour camp

parched
Serengeti.

L. S. Klatt Poet Laureate of Grand Rapids, Michigan

Silo

Long ago, I got
hold of a farm. I
blew the daylights
out of it. Acres of
alfalfa incinerated;
the silo in which
Demeter was lifted
up & from which one
could see Pluto; &
the tractor, creature
of habit. I was
happy to abide
underground in a
fallout shelter that
reinforced my fear
of the future. Phrase
of a meadowlark
I remembered there.
Cold water stream where
crayfish lay dreamy, in
this I immersed. Once
in a blue moon, I
would walk a country
mile. It was enough.

damian lopes Poet Laureate of Barrie, Ontario

kandahar time

for JJ & the BBs, 2009

1

snow crunches under foot
right at the intersection
past my son & his friend

silent flakes
blur the little house
on the corner

despite curtains drawn
it beckons
through crisp air

the drive shoveled
grey asphalt
dusted with snow

finer
than the neglected walk
we trudge

the van warms in the drive
brushed & scraped
wipers intermittent

from the corner hydrant
the front door open
behind storm glass

in his car seat
the baby plays
with his toes

beyond your
shadow flits between
the older two

& again i regret
not leaving five minutes earlier
a moment in my day

because
i don't know the time
in kandahar

2

how do i feel your tremble
as you stand steady
hands buried to cuffs
in pant pockets

your eyes equally
steadfast confidence
betrayed
by them

awkward &

fearing offence
you beg a hug
an adult's contact

& i am touched
unfamiliar my arms
enfold you gladly
offer what i am

so much smaller than
your husband but for
eleven thousand kilometres
southeast

3

neighbours congregate
to sign & colour your banner
to encircle trunks
branches posts & poles

guiding beacons
divali lamps of
yellow ribbons
down the street

tied by hand they
disappear
in the breadth of this
quiet road

alone
we guess the route

you will drive home
after this long

fear weather
will disparage bows
or darkness
hide them from you

4

the little house on holgate
where my wife caught
all three of your boys
is still white

but the trikes & toys
are gone

Martin Achatz Poet Laureate of the Upper Peninsula, Michigan

Waiting for Independence Day Fireworks 2013

On this July 4,
a girl with pink hair
wrestles a pit bull
in the grass as Black Pearl
plays "Stand by Me"
on the bandstand.
The sky touches the ground
with a wide palm
of sun, day clinging
to these last suckling moments,
nursing dusk's green milk.
So much skin and tattoo around,
flesh against flesh.
I smell coconut
from a flock of teenage
girls who whisper and giggle by,
Budweiser and Marlboros
from the boys close behind them.
An old man and woman sit
in lawn chairs to my left,
eat bratwurst, watch
kids loft Frisbees into the darkening
air. When she's down
to her last bite, the old woman
reaches over, feeds it
to the old man, who accepts it,
kisses her fingertips, his lips
smeared with mustard.
Two men appear.

One carries a blanket.
Their hands almost touch
as they walk together.
They spread their blanket
on the ground, the way
my mom and dad
used to spread towels
on the beach in August,
without need for word
or direction, an easy ballet
of arm and hand, crouch,
kneel, an act they'd repeated
so many times it gleamed
like a rock in lake shallows,
polished for years by tides, waves.
Everyone pauses as the men
sit close to each other,
gray heads like twin dandelions
sprouting from a single weed.
They talk, laugh, drink beer
from brown, long-necked bottles.
Soon, everyone forgets
to be shocked
as night overtakes us,
makes us all the same, ·
one crowd, indivisible,
under stars and moon,
our bodies primed
for the freedom to love
the sky any way we want.

Aliki Barnstone Missouri Poet Laureate (grew up in Bloomington, Indiana)

Fire on the Waters

On one of our road-trips we stopped
on the shore of Lake Erie, a beach
of smooth slate gray rocks.

Handing us a few of the flattest ones,
my dad taught us how to skip stones
across the Erie's surface, making

only the thinnest ripples on the silver
waters reaching into a distant silver
horizon barely distinct from the sky,

"too silver for a seam," no green
tree-lined shore in sight, so vast
is even a smaller Great Lake's expanse.

That might have been before
the 1969 Cuyahoga River Fire
spread onto Lake Erie, dead

from sewage and industrial waste.
I remember fish bones and feathers
among the slick stones and mud,

my little brother triumphantly holding
up a long quill, maybe an eagle's
or a hawk's, and my mother shouting
"Put that down!" and "Don't touch!"

Joel Lipman Poet Laureate of Lucas County, Ohio

Code Word

TEACH TOLERANCE

"Bias is learned early, often at home. Schools can offer lessons in tolerance and acceptance. Host a diversity and inclusion day on campus. Reach out to young people who may be susceptible to hate group propaganda and prejudice."

Siduri Beckman Philadelphia Youth Poet Laureate

Trouble Writing

I think I've been having so much trouble writing, so stuck, so blank
      Because I know what I should write// the words I want to write//
      the things that
      People entrust poets with because sometimes we keep words like gifts

To tuck under your tongue.

      Last month I was standing in a room of second graders,
      My room of second graders but less West Philadelphia now than it
was when I played double dutch on the blacktop
And They showed me their black and white paper cutouts of Dr. King
Waving him in the air, like a flag of academic progress
So my teacher, their teacher asks me to ask them: What did Dr. King do?

I don't—I realized—I don't know how he did it. So I ask them:

What did Dr. King do?

He wrote letters. He gave speeches. He didn't fight. Three word sentences.
Three word tracks.
They know, who fought back.

Why did he write? I ask. Why did he march?

Pulling abstractions from second graders why not write my own
How can I be one
to put pen to paper in the shadow of giants who carry words to change
nations

What sense of the world can I bring smashed between 45th and Locust
Between Mayor and Major
Between Penn and West Philadelphia
Between Mother and Father

My mother never promised me anything from this country said it was full
of liars and thieves that the art that prevailed was what kept us from falling
back into the darkness that was the

American family.

My father promised me I could reap everything from this country that I
could put my feet in the cracks and climb to the top if I shed a little maybe a
little dignity or worry I would fly.

My mother is an immigrant but she is
English/white/educated.
My father was unemployed but with
degrees from Cornell/Cambridge/Princeton/Yale.

We were an American family.

I wonder what I would score on the Philadelphia Children's PTSD test.

I would get one point for a divorce.
I have never seen anyone die. never gone without food. never actively feared
for my life not one single time and yet
here I am writing about what it means to fight, just because
I am a Philadelphian, just because
I thought I understood my privilege, yet my sub
conscious forced a hiatus, stopped my tongue before it ran away with ideals
of liberty for my country

That I too, loved.

The second graders wanted something from me. among them sat a lanky brother a late child and
somehow some part mine.

We have a German name—Iowanized—Americanized—Anglicized so write it down in the cursive print of our country in English in our school in our home in our privilege and try to dig out what that name could mean, where it could have gone, who wore it, what they did with it, how they cut it, how they broke it

How we taste it, how we hold it
How we wear it.

Could I do that? I sister. I gather. I pick up in my arms all the loves I feel between the tops and sides of different people and
            one day I could pull faces together and we would all sleep at night instead of stare like wonder at the things we didn't say.

one day two tongues can cross in livery and

one will bite back.

I want to teach my brother to push out the words where there are none
But also to highlight
what has been said
Marginalized words// what we are saying is not novel not unspoken
to see silence as a whole// to see his silence as a tool and employ it
to step back so that Americans can claim their own movements
Step back without stepping out
Step up to shift out 1789// 1866// 1919// 1971 words.

My mother isn't bleak she wants me to know that
she really does believe in the glory and mystery of life.

I choose to stay in Philadelphia.

The magic lies in the reframing so tell the second graders to write for the world
And they just might.

Karla Huston Wisconsin Poet Laureate

Tempting Mystery

How can I show this child the way
to write about war? She's never seen
more than what's been shown on tv:

the blown footage, the bodiless flags,
iridescent missiles arcing in some foreign
night, while bullets whistle

across a thirty-six inch screen.
She's never tasted sand, acrid with smoke,
touched mud studded with bones,

or seen blood blacken as it dries.
She's never known the smell of a corpse
or how it fills her mouth with vomit.

Still she understands the big picture,
the waste and suffering, burnt
offerings to political gods.

To her, death is a tempting mystery,
so how can I tell her what loss means?
She must imagine war as more

than just busted buildings on yellowed paper,
more than six o'clock sound bites.
She must hunt for the wounded,

seek the man with no eyes, the woman
with a hole in her heart,
the boy too dumbed to speak.

Thomas O'Connell Poet Laureate of Beacon, New York

Foreshadowing Means Nothing to Us Kids

We made armies
Or ourselves
Hiding behind trees
And pointing sticks at each other

We watched movies
And believed
Our boys always won
Marching proudly in the parade

Watched my mother
As she paused
Giving a dollar
Outside of the supermarket
Cloth forget-me-nots tied around the rear view mirror

Yolanda Wisher Poet Laureate of Montgomery County, Pennsylvania

diversity day

i brought the palestinian woman's poem to the diversity day planning
meeting at 3:15pm. the poem's smell filled the room with zaatar & burning
flesh & the risk of the palestinian woman's voice from a podium on diversity
day became too great. i felt my face start to freeze, the way it knows how,
over time, to scorn cracking; my black coarsening from the bowels. pacing
thoughts of june, black thru & thru in the deepest, darkest ways like audre;
yeah, thought of june, black girl from cali, like alice, like lucille, like sonia,
claiming palestine, claiming *everywhere*. claiming human & all its hussiness,
i learned my common sense from these seers, little-known thru & thru at
the diversity day table. so when they started talkin about african drums
& sing-a-longs & *nice* poets, i felt myself beginning to boil like glaciers
waking up evil from elemental pasts. i left the room in a hot piss of words,
walked through the germantown the quaker ladies be afraid of, my mother's
freedom-songs cut up like a dj's samplin in my head. to home base, to sit
with the rain on the third floor, to untangle the knot in my pretty little neck
from an invisible noose.

Yolanda Wisher Poet Laureate of Montgomery County, Pennsylvania

blues & vision for PS whatever

2015

ridin the train
we pass buildings
with busted eyes
& rotted mouths.
at night, kids play
the fame game here.

all the schools
are empty-headed
all the principals are broke.
some smoke dope
& it's like *shawshank redemption*
in these schools.
it's like *12 years a slave*
up in these schools.
it's like lupita
never been discovered
gettin banged up
in the bathroom
on her way to the GED.
can't nobody
afford college no more.
a scholarship
is a short joke.
the college prep
is just a hustle,
up in these schools.

cuz it's like *amistad*
up in these schools.
some lost, burnt out teachers
in these schools.
yellin at babies at 8am
in the morning in these schools
& the brother is right:
it's a charade
an elaborate maze
it's like *scandal*
up in these schools.
gladiator rings &
daily tests of the spirit.
it's like *the book of eli*
up in these schools.

it's like you & me
sleepin dumb at the wheel
while the rats & rocks
raise our babies up,
to be, that's right,
rats & rocks.
it's like that.

2035

flyin with our third eyes,
we pass tiny homes
nestled in urban forests
voluptuous community gardens
art parks. at night,
kids gather here
for free college
courses & concerts.

all the schools
are two-headed
& all the principals
are gurus.
some can levitate
& it's like *a different world*
in these schools.
it's like *daughters of the dust*
up in these schools.
it's like janelle monae gets
discovered everyday,
buys moonland with her reparations
& starts buildin the q.u.e.e.ncraft.
& everybody
can afford college
'cause it's free
& the college prep
is survival skills, like
how to light a fire
in your mind
how to find your self
without a GPS or SAT.
cuz it's like *purple rain*
& *beat street*
up in these schools.
it's teachers who be
artists & activists
up in these schools.
graduation masquerade balls
poetry slams in the cafeteria
sky labyrinths for gym class
dance classes for detention
it's like the *buena vista social club*
up in these schools.
it's like *space is the place*

up in these schools.

& it's like you & me
wakin up at the wheel
while the horizon washes
over our heads
& our eyelashes grow
into wings & fly out
ahead of our eyes.
it's like you & me
dreamin up these schools.
it's like that.

Thomas Leduc Poet Laureate of Sudbury, Ontario

Paper Dolls

I want her to be more,
more than a handful
of lines in a movie,
all of which are about a boy.
More than the commodity
of a half-dressed pop-star.
More than a stressed out
house wife with nowhere to go.
More than the pretty paper dolls
she has placed so perfectly
before her on the kitchen tiles,
two dimensional women
half naked and exposed
picture perfect models,
designing her, as much
as she is dressing them.
She's learning
and my hands are bound
and papercut.

225

Samuel Hazo Pennsylvania Poet Laureate

For Which It Stands

Crosswinds have slashed the flag
   so that the thirteenth ribbon
   dangles free or coils around
   the flagpole like a stripe.
                    What's left
keeps fluttering in red-and-white
defiance.
          Somehow the tattering
seems apropos.
              The President
proclaims we'll be at war forever—
not war for peace but war
upon war, though hopefully not here.
Believers in eternal re-election
   hear his pitch and pray.
                In Washington
God's lawyer warns we stand
at Armageddon, and we battle
for the Lord.
             Elsewhere, California's
governor believes in California's
governor, and football bowls
are named for Mastercard, Pacific
Life, Con-Agra and Tostitos.
Out west a plan to gerrymander
   Colorado (Texas-style) fails,
   but barely.
            Asked why no flag
is studded in his coat lapel

or decorates his aerial, a veteran
responds, "I wear my flag
on my heart—I don't wear
my heart on my sleeve."
                              Today
for once we're spared the names
of occupying soldiers shot
or rocketed to fragments in Iraq.
Collateral damage?
                    Two boys,
their mother and both grandparents.
No names for them.
                    Just Arabs.

Larry Jensen Poet Laureate of Owen Sound, Ontario

This Great Lake Town

By the Great Lake water
There's a Great Lake town
Where the cliffs of Niagara
Weave through and around
Where the green of the valley
Hugs the blue of the sound
Where it's hard and it's easy
In this Great Lake town

Built on the backs
Of the ones before
On the tracks by the water
And the factory floor
And from the hard rock soil
And the fishing ground
From the blood and the toil
In this Great Lake town

From my own time present
And sometime before
The sons and the fathers
Came home from the war
Forever changed and damaged
From the world they had found
That too is the making
Of this Great Lake town

Now my own daughter
And her daughters and son

Are by this body of water
The very same one
That's held me and freed me
Kept my feet on this ground
Spell bound by the beauty
Of this Great Lake town

Rodney Torreson Poet Laureate of Grand Rapids, Michigan

The Brooder House Rabbits

"Unless a statute requires that the neglect be malicious, it doesn't matter that someone accused of neglecting animals didn't intend to be cruel."

—Mary Randolph, J.D., Nolo.com

At first our hands lapped waves
of fur, while their ears, long on patience,
heard out our silken hearts.
From their hutches, we gave them
over to their kind in an old
brooder house, where they bred quickly
without design, 4 becoming 70,
surely 100 if they stood to be counted,
each doe lunging into her own gut
for fur to cover the bobbing
sausages twitching out noses and ears.
Some reared to full-size in a weekend,
gaunt and wild of daylight,
grinding teeth, lungs bucking dust,
the same rabbit sometimes
doubling, so it could blame us
for its plight from two places at once.

Each day my brother and I
picked up stiff corpses,
our bodies a constant moving hearse.
The air always lame, we failed
to heal them through water—medicine
stirred in. And so, we came less and

less often with coffee cans
of water and pellets. The overflow
of containers said forget them:
there was nothing we could do.
When, finally, we'd show, skeletons
thumped a back leg of warning.
We were the monsters,
and their little eye holes
dared us to sink the worms
of our fingers in.

Liz Zetlin Poet Laureate of Owen Sound, Ontario

Ground Truthing on her twentieth day

Looks like I've missed my morning fix of sleeping baby. All
I see on the webcam are the crinkles of sheet where she lay.
Sun shines through the crib slats casting bars of light and
shadow. A luminous ball of white appears, creating a comet
with a long tail.

I browse the news—stumble upon a scientist who found
a scary change in Greenland's albedo, the amount of light
reflected by a surface. *When sunlight hits a glacier,* he says,
*most of it bounces back into space, instead of being absorbed
by dark-blue oceans or green forests. But not all ice shines with
the same brightness.* The comet's head in her crib elongates,
intensifies.

*As snow crystals warm—even before they melt—they lose their
jagged edges and become rounder, reflecting less light. Think
of the way wet sand is darker than dry sand.* A cloud passes
over her crib.

This summer, *without warning, the line on the albedo
chart dropped deep into uncharted territory.* The scientist's
heart skips a beat, doubts the data. So he does a "ground-
truthing"—going out on the land. He sees the ice sheet itself
is darkening. *Greenland,* he writes, *is a sleeping giant that's
waking.* Her crib is still empty. The comet has disappeared,
leaving the sheet grey, absorbing more light.

This is the kind of moment, at least in geologic terms, that marks the grand tidal changes of history. Her comet reappears, its head now shaped like a megaphone.

I shake off images of the silent metamorphosis of ice crystals, of all hell breaking loose, and bring to mind the profound love on the faces of her mom and dad and all those who melt in her orbit, for all newborns shine with a crystalline brightness, one small body at a time.

quotes from "The Arctic Ice Crisis" by Bill McKibben, from the August 30, 2012, issue of *Rolling Stone*

David Helwig Poet Laureate of Prince Edward Island (born in Toronto, Ontario)

Walt Whitman on the TTC

"In Toronto at half-past one. I rode up on top of the omnibus with the driver. The city made the impression on me of a lively dashing place. The lake gives it its character." —Walt Whitman, diary entry, July 26–27, 1880

The track of buses along and back, the pattern
of many-miles-streets where one suburb stumbles
into another, east travelling west, west to east,
south north, all tied together by streetcars, subway,
creeks filled in, the lake far off, invisible.
Houses side by side shape the neighbourhood,
always its daily sequence, the years of travel,
morning's departure, afternoon's return,
nights of poetry, the dangerous dreams.

At the bus stop the arms and legs of grown girls
in uniforms of light and dark grace the air.
Did you? Did she? Did he? Did they really?
The red passenger coach swings to the curb
and we enter, the driver in his seat checking
tickets, passes, transfers. We wait, sway
with the steering of the long bus, lurch at the juncture,
the red light. *Did you hear? Did she? Did he?*
West travelling east, east to west, north south.

Sudden as noisy migrant waterfowl
the flock of maturing girls rises to depart:
Thank you, Goodbye, driver, Goodbye, Thanks;
the red bus swings into traffic, words
cross the excited street, swerve, vanish.

Gail Bellamy Poet Laureate of Cleveland Heights, Ohio

Imagination is Your First History Teacher

If you think political fundraisers suck,
imagine yourself in the 1700s, after dinner
but before The Revolution (pick one)
Fortunately you passed up those
putrefying green-tinged pheasant slices
but nevertheless you're itching, taking wispy
breaths in a tight corset, prostrated by
menstrual cramps yet perched on
a tiny needlepoint-covered chair
in a yellow music room,
listening to variations
on a Mozart minuet
the harpsichord in jolly contrast
to what's going on in your life
on this rainy night
with lightning fighting the
flickering tapers of the candelabras
During a rest you think you hear the faint
tuning of a violin—no, several
violins—just beyond the green
baize door, and a deep throat-clearing

Deborah Cooper Poet Laureate of Duluth, Minnesota

Talking to Strangers

An old man
in a coffee shop
in Nipigon

tells me stories
of his childhood

the year his family lived
inside a chicken coop

the smell his mother
couldn't bleach away

the way it lingered
in their clothes.

They ate oatmeal
twice a day

bowing their heads
for grace

Bless us, O Lord,
and these Thy gifts

and once,
on Christmas Eve

outside the door,
bounty of oranges.

Three a piece

the small boy
still there,
in his eyes

and one for Mum.

Liz Zetlin Poet Laureate of Owen Sound, Ontario

The Warnings

> *These are the warnings*
> *that you must forget*
> *if you're climbing out of yourself.*
> *If you're going to smash into the sky.*
> —Anne Sexton, *Riding the Elevator into the Sky*

Do not cling to the you
you are supposed to be.
The one your parents called
trouble or *shy* or *good*.
Do not let others limit you
with their longings.
Don't wait for the right time,
the last call, the most
beautiful of mornings.
These are the warnings.

Our hearts receive them
and our minds discount.
Each day we turn up
the machinery of judgment
and each day we struggle
most with what's not yet.
We have a hard time not
hoping for something else
because there is a bad debt
that you must forget.

Remember compassion
first for yourself and then
for all beings until
you cannot bear not
to help others reach
past themselves
into a crowd of clouds
because you have to climb
far from the continental shelf
if you're climbing out of yourself.

This is it. This *is* it
and *it* will change.
This is what I tell myself.
You have to practise
like a mountain climber
who's not afraid to fall
or like a singer with a sore throat
who braves the highest notes.
All this is born in the mind's eye
if you're going to smash into the sky.

Yolanda Wisher Poet Laureate of Montgomery County, Pennsylvania

blues for PS whatever 2

the children have lost their baby smells. you sneeze. but you still come in close to read over their lines. the young poet with the unleashed, unadorned body odor is waging a weapon against all of us, the audience. there is no pretty font for funk. is it their bodies or their clothes that smell so mean? the children reek of indifference. the smell will linger if you grab ahold of one of them. the smell will stay with you like malik's frankincense. it will hang about you like a spy or a stalker. it makes you funky & enraged as hendrix or the godfather, don't it? it makes you blacker to hug the child who reeks of blind indifference. a stank that's funny, cruel now, dangerous later. it'll get in you, that's what you think, it'll get in you if you let the caress of children last long enough. that funk is why you break out early, why you let go first. your nose is mounting a defensive & you roll on to the next kid with his phrase about the spider web or her three lines about the butterflies & the backpack that smells like a joint smoked two centuries ago. there's a haiku on the board & it's far from funky. it's clean & white in a japanese kind of way. you teach the children to meditate like gurus in their own funk. you, on the other hand, are still learning.

Joel Lipman Poet Laureate of Lucas County, Ohio

mistakes

DIG DEEPER

"Tolerance, fundamentally, is a personal decision. It comes from an attitude that is learnable and embraceable: a belief that every voice matters, that all people are valuable, that no one is 'less than'. . . Look inside yourself for prejudices and stereotypes. Build your own cultural competency, then keep working to expose discrimination wherever it happens—in housing, employment, education, and more."

Sarah Sadie (Busse) Poet Laureate of Madison, Wisconsin

A Poem Does Invite

> A poem does invite, it does require. What does it invite? A poem invites you
> to feel. More than that: it invites you to respond. And better than that: a poem
> invites a total response. —Muriel Rukeyser, The Life of Poetry

Rilke was right. Rukeyser, right. The total
response: change your life. It's night,
it's (finally) winter, season of ice and delight.

Season of darkness and wild.
Here in Chicago, America, ice storm and all
the angles of steel, our forward momentum. Two girls

play where I cannot see them, only hear
their chatter and giggles, lit and warm and electric.
Soon, I will walk them both home, out through the sleet,

will watch them running ahead, sliding and darting
and slipping delightedly on in the night,
through uncalendared possibilities.

And what is my role, except witness? Just like those girls,
the cursors, jittery verticals, move by fits
and starts; the nib of my pen scratches this white

expanse, piercing and drawing out, line
by line, defining the deeper shadows. "If
there is a feeling that something has been lost,

it may be because much has not yet been used,
much is still to be found and begun." Muriel,
self-described She-poet, you roar and purr by turns,

equally fierce at the start and at the end.
Reading your words I feel my teeth grow.
I have accepted too much. And too little.

Sandra Fees Poet Laureate of Berks County, Pennsylvania

After Dr. Bonganjalo Goba's Death

In class he queried us:
what gets you up in the morning?

I craved a reply worthy
of what he believed we

could each be for the other
urgent as a liberated thing

such as a flight of crows
or children at recess.

Now at night I startle awake.
Padding down the hall,

white rectangles cast themselves
across the rug like piano tiles.

My eyes seek the source
and pierce layers

of glass and a brittle web
of magnolia branches

to catch the gibbous moon
adrift like a pale balloon.

I want to tell him
I get up for the promised

light-fullness of this:
a life well used.

Shari Wagner Indiana Poet Laureate

The farm wife receives a certified letter

It's from an Esquire in Chicago.
"Sincerely yours," he tells us,

but I see, between the lines,
how he wants to raze the barn

and turn over the garden for good.
The trees where my daughters played

house in the branches would vanish.
The creek where cows grazed

would be drainage. Behind his desk
this man expands the production

of boxed-up piglets who never own
a waking hour to wallow in sunlight.

My terse Grandma Iva was wise
as a serpent and innocent as a dove.

I know what she would write:
"What you do is what you become."

Sandra Fees Poet Laureate of Berks County, Pennsylvania

Keeping Time at the Family Detention Center

His face unchanging
the guard catalogs Christmas gifts
as though a toy helicopter
or wristwatch are contraband
and returns the silver watch
its ivory face and Arabic numerals
prohibited from keeping time
within the faceless brick walls
of Family Detention
where a Salvadoran boy
counts days and his mother
counts years

is makeup okay? I ask

because his mother
wants to make herself over
for the shimmery release
that awaits her and her son
who loves math
and folds origami paper
into orange and pink cranes
to multiply the dream of flight

yes but no compacts with mirrors, replies the guard

my reflection
hovers in the window
a veil of whiteness

above the guard's shoulder
and beyond the glass
empty playground swings dangle
while afternoon light casts
slivery shards
to pierce the façade.

Sandra Fees Poet Laureate of Berks County, Pennsylvania

Asylum Thwarted

What would Anna Akhmatova
say, she who could describe
the frightening years
waiting in prison queues
in rain-gray Leningrad
two years before my birth
in a country I may never see?

What would rise in her mouth
like trees grown whole overnight
planted first in her songbird breast
branches outstretching
the vastness of grief
to name what must be named
in any age in any nation?

How can I invoke her words
to rise again in my mouth
in the shape of trees
to describe the years
when something called *asylum*
failed to take root in the pursed lips
of my country majesty of the beautiful

in the isolating years
as I wait
outside these detention center doors
in rain-gray Pennsylvania

to visit Salvadoran mothers and children
who appeal for a postlude
to this song of requiem?

Pauletta Hansel Poet Laureate of Cincinnati, Ohio

On Grief: November 2016

I.

The 6th stage of grief
is *meaning*, says the man
who ought to know, the one
up at the death and dying podium
who flies around the country
fueled by our tears.
I like this guy.
He says no matter how rich
the meaning, it is
never worth the cost.
But we're a meaning-making animal,
(that's me talking now) always
searching for some reason,
as if this unnatural
disaster of a president-elect
will turn out to be
the push-to-the-cliff-edge
this country needed, or maybe
it's how Mary meets Bob, or Barb
or Miguel at the No Trump March
and the kid they'll raise
will cure dementia
someday, but too late
for my mother,
or Ronald Reagan,
or our country,
and maybe for me,

if Mom has the kind
that runs in the family,
after all.

     II.

Back at the nursing home,
the shriveled lady whose dementia
is resting on a step or two
before my mom's
looks over the table at us
as my fingers slip some bits of fruit
between my mother's lips
and asks, *Who has your heart?*
I'd say it's pretty obvious, which maybe
is her point, or maybe not. My mother
doesn't have my heart, not literally,
but I read on the internet
(therefore it must be true)
that fetal cells remain
inside the mother's body
all her life, and so she may
have me in her heart,
or in her spleen,
or a bit of me floating around
her withering brain,
which might explain
how she can tell me, sometimes,
what I had for dinner,
or who just died, or that the apples
we bought from the market
aren't worth the cost.

III.

The principles of grief work,
the grief guy declares,
are say goodbye
to who they were, start new
with whoever they are now.
And my mother and I
are doing pretty well,
at least today,
with our comingling cells
but I don't think
I will be making nice
with the country we're about to get.
It's *Bedtime for Bonzo*
all over again,
except without directors
or a script
and the contract on America
has been renewed,
this time as unreality television.
The last TV show I really liked
was *Buffy the Vampire Slayer*
from way back when the other
Clinton was in office. I know
I'm not the only one;
just last week I saw a rusting Toyota
with the bumper sticker,
What Would Buffy Do?
She'd kick some ass,
that's what. I'm going to
stick with anger,
stage two.

Jim Ferris Poet Laureate of Lucas County, Ohio

Contagious

Pat Cahill, Pat
    Cahill, Pat,
I hope I was not
    an asshole
to you when we were snotty
    little angels
in near orb. I probably
    was—I thought
I walked better than you,
    there but
for the grace of God—
    I left you
the way they left me,
    as if that
excuses anything,
    catch me if
you can, we learn from all
    the wrong people,
cripples can't afford to be seen
    together,
CP is scary, spasms
    are scary,
make the sign of the cross
    and say
an Our Father and a Hail
    Mary,
two miserable stumbling losers
    is a gang,

a vortex of threat, horror,
     and shame—
it's not contagious,
     is it? Mamas,
yank your babies back
     from this event
horizon—no one outweighs
     the afflicted child,
these smart, funny kids,
     these smart-ass
kids who walk funny,
     why can't you
be a good little cripple
     like Pat, say hello,
Pat, must not let the poor
     misfortunates
compound their problems,
     it's bad
enough as it is.

What you knew, Pat Cahill,
     boy seer,
they look to us in fear,
     we're not
supposed to see—
     we are not
alone forever, dust
     and ice specks
wandering some dim sad
     dwarf galaxy—
we could have told each other:
     all this
is temporary, we
     already

shine like planets, our gravity
    unavoidable.
I hope I was not
    an asshole
to you, brother—not
    even once.

Howard D. Paap Poet Laureate of Bayfield, Wisconsin

A Life Reborn

Back in the day
The Ojibwe language
Was the lingua franca
In Lake Superior Country
Spoken by the Whites
And Native alike.

Those Jesuits had to learn it
Three hundred years ago
Before they could tell of their god.
It was the fur trader's tongue
Even the visiting Dakota
When in times of peace
And coming to The Bay
Struggled to handle its vowels.

But then came civilization.

Strange how things happen,
How with time's passing
A language can come alive again
As the power of the words
Awakes the land's old truth.

So today, in Ojibwe Country,
The people's tongue
Is sought after, has awakened
From its hundred year sleep
To be heard again.

Now classes appear like songbirds in spring.
And those with the golden tongues
In whose blood the old words
Had been sleeping for a generation or two,
Those with the minds so quick
Are speaking that language of old,
That lingua franca of the New Time.

To hear that tongue again,
To see what it does
As The People respond,
As they walk a little taller
Greeting each other in the old way.

Tomorrow at the first hint of dawn
Go to the lake and listen.
You will feel it in the morning wind,
Hear it in the first calls of the water
Coming alive after its long night of sleep.

Shari Wagner Indiana Poet Laureate

The Rhoads Family

"Perhaps the most exciting event connected with the Underground Railroad in this vicinity was the attempt to capture and carry back to slavery a family named Rhoads." —*Our Westfield, 1834–1984*

On the moonless night they escaped
Singleton Vaughn set loose
a bloodhound shadow
that tracked them from Missouri,
across the foggy Mississippi,
to Indiana Quakers. John chinked
their cabin water-tight
and refused to add a window,
but that shadow sniffed the yard,
wouldn't budge, had them treed.

He kept an axe beside the bed,
but axes can't slice through shadows
and in his nightmares this one
grew shaggy and ran with a pack
over silent, frozen fields.

When the knock came, a thunderclap
shaking him awake, John leapt
to the bolted door, grasping the axe.
Rhuann held the children
as Vaughn's shadow panted sour
breath near their necks.

When the roof creaked,
she stoked the chimney with chairs
and bed slats, pine needle batting,
even the houseboat John whittled
for the children—Noah
and his family inside.

Just as the fire sputtered
and Rhuann was adding the last chapter
of a Bible she'd been learning to read,
dawn poked a branch
under the door
and she told the family to muster
a voice no slave would use.

A boy on the road heard the shouts.
He saw two wolves at the chimney,
another at the door
and dropped his school books
to dash to other farms
till what gathered
was a flock armed with nothing
but what Friends were holding
when they heard the call—a hay rake
or a rolling pin.

When John opened the door,
all that light swooped in
so potent it washed Mr. Vaughn
back to Missouri
where his hungry shadow
hounded him.

John B. Lee Poet Laureate of Brantford and Norfolk County, Ontario

He tells me

he tells me
of an ancient burial mound
on the northern shores
of Superior—his Ojibwa ancestors
lacing their bones in the earth
reaching through life
like the most common roots of lives once lived

he tells me
in the war
of the confederacy
of the three fires
how his people
tore the arms and legs
away from the corpses
of the vanquished Iroquois
how they decapitated these foe
burning their longhouses scouring their villages
how they scattered
disfigured bodies
like a whirlwind come to a fractured forest

so that in the afterlife
they might not
gather back the spirits
of the fallen and unenduring enemy

their souls tattered
like rain-torn smoke

thinned to nothing by bad weather
and the hissing away of wet burn

he tells me
his grandfather's great grandfather
was once a war chief
in that old
victory over time
that comes to the knowing

and last evening
in the late afternoon before our talk
I walked
my local streets
down Richardson past Aaron
left onto Denby
to Mergyl then home
along Nelson
and it was such a lovely
leaf-whipped autumn
perhaps the last
of the good days
before winter
lost faith with the sun
and I saw
one leaf rise
out of the bustling multitude
catching itself
like something solitary
something joyful
in the multifarious hordes
of vanquished beauty

and comes home memory

comes home dream
and I would think of this
unblooming
this shattering sky
even as this good man
tells me
his own heroic story
of the doomed ghosts of a glorious war

and I hope
I am also that
one lonesome leaf
lifting its voice
through blue silence
and drifting off into darkness
yet to come
miles from the fire
catching my feet
in the crimson rumour of this dying hour
when the spirit
of every broken thing
finds an everlasting champion
gone ahead, left behind
and quietly waiting

George Elliott Clarke Canadian Parliamentary Poet Laureate

À Rimini

I.

From Ravenna to Rimini—
from Duke of one to Duke the next—
from paternal Duke to husbandly Duke—

pass I, from Ravenna to Rimini—
to make a marriage Machiavellian,
to imp *Concord* upon conflicting dukes.

No one cares for, curries favour with, me—
slave
to a papa's policy:
To ally with a once-upon-a-time lecher,
pay court to his twisted mouth and poxy hands,
just to unlatch his gold-pregnant purse.

Life—that *Sleep*-adulterated *Fancy*—
is, for every woman,
an eventual assignation with *Degradation*.

Thus, I passed to a man
ruing the ruin that's his downturned sex—
his disease-damaged sex—

but wedding him by proxy,

via his vigorous brother, Paolo—

startlingly handsome

&

depressingly penniless.

  II.

But *Nature* overthrows vows:

Sedulously, unhurriedly, I introduced
the Duke's palimpsest sex—

his brother's (Paolo's)—

to my own.

I shan't credit this conjunction
"adulterous,"
for, in the wedding ceremony
Paolo did stand in, gamely,

for his brother,
Duke Giovanni di Rimini,

and, as a stand-up stand-in,
stood out, aptly,
in ending my incomplete *Womanhood,*

by being manly,
wherein Duke Giovanni was a *Mirage* . . . .

And how could I love a portrait—
though it be hung above my bed?

III.

I'm not like that Sicilian virgin
and her mama,

who yielded to doubled ruffians
who doubly, penetrating both fiancé and dame,
plugged, repetitively,
six sexualized vents

only half an hour before the gowned bride
vowed, "I do,"

weeping for what witnesses thought was *Joy*,
when it was genuine *Woe*.

No, I'd not have my bridal bed furnished
with a pillow of daggers.

IV.

I came to Rimini—
through days of rain and mud—
a swamp landscape
of sequined waves.
My broken feelings
brought me a waste physique.

This palace's rooms
indulged groomed *Silence*.
I feared I'd grow old,
studying the uncanny
architecture of vines,

or waves' tottering *Violence*.

I wandered the beach,
inconsequential,
amazed I wasn't yet
already flotsam—
a decrepit, sodden,
melting paper valentine.

It's not Paolo's fault—
or a *Sin* or a *Crime*—
that I lusted after
the scrambled breathing
of honest couples,
ignorant of *Statecraft*.

My supposèd husband—
Giovanni—as haughty,
austere, and fearsome
as a guillotine—
was mulish and mawkish,
forbidding us *amore*.

V.

Paolo delivered sweaty arguments—
groaning velvet—
sheets of moonlight,
a body not a painting,

a scissor of flesh,

scalding moments as brilliant as gold.

But Duke Giovanni finally came,
campaigning home to his claim,

and got me down in bed
as he vainly "got it up,"

but could only emit a jack-off smell,

rancid, regrettable,

and I knew I didn't, couldn't, ever love
the unmanly man,

stink of limoncello out his nostrils;
his capillaries clogged with booze.

So, in my sleep, craving Paolo,
I cried his name,

and Giovanni went from our bed
to his drowsy bro's,
and ran his sword through my own Adam,
belly to ass,

to render his palace body
a maggot toilet.

Never again would I feel velvet sweat,
arguments of groans,
or a column of silk
plungering my sex.

VI.

Starved for Paolo's honey,
I threw myself down a well.

Then Dante totted up our history—

placing us, embracing still, in Hell.

[Barcelona (Spain) *la Saint-Valentin* mmxv]

Sheila Packa Poet Laureate of Duluth, Minnesota

Dialectics

assembled from Hegel and Marx

Water to ice.
A change in the nature of a thing.
To go beyond appearances to reality.
To see with my own eyes, to hear, to think
to speak a language of becoming.
Change is old, a mole
burrowing underground unseen for a long time
that suddenly emerges into the light.
The ground shifts, the surface turns over.
Never anywhere is there matter without motion.
Winter turns to spring.
To reach into the past for the future.
A chain of changes.
A trigger. A catalyst. A strike.
Propelled by being held back.
Negation of the negation.
To become what I was not.
Contradiction makes motion possible.
Inseparable are causes and effects.
The river without beginnings or ends.
One thing forms and the opposite reforms.
Progress proceeds through a series of contradictions.
The shattering of the old
a sudden overturn.

273

Sarah Sadie (Busse) Poet Laureate of Madison, Wisconsin

If Only

If only we would remember
we're animals, soft in our needs.
If only we could make peace
with the fact of our bones.
I keep a small pile of teeth,
my daughter's, beside my mirror.
Not all of them, but the last few,
kept once I learned about time.

I say to you,
a woman is her own
wild source in this world.
Touch deep to find that small,
burrowed self that sleeps through arid winter.
Trust. The thaw will come in its time,
and we will breathe that new element bravely.

I use *woman* in the universal
sense of the word, of course.
I use *daughter* in the universal
sense of the world.

Laurence Sansone Poet Laureate of Beacon, New York

20 Percent

Let gentlemen everywhere, just for a day,
For all they consume and for each dollar spent,
Take out a small portion and throw it away.
Not much off the top, only 20 percent.

On lavishment, luxury, leisure and meals,
Hold back bare necessities, groceries, rent,
Spend that amount lesser to see how it feels.
What strain? Don't complain! It's just 20 percent.

Take time off your phone calls with family and friends,
Tear out the back pages you haven't yet read,
Walk out on a film without seeing the end,
You missed out on something? That's 20 percent.

Decrease all your volume and dim all the lights,
Turn taps, tighten knobs, limit gears, narrow vents,
Take in shallow breaths, keep your bladder held tight,
It burns? Now you're learning 'bout 20 percent.

Now let's make a toast, raise your cracked glasses high,
The fissure will dribble all which represents,
What every last woman you know in your life,
Receives less than you. That's right, 20 percent.

So, just in case you haven't figured by now,
What makes this unfair, and begun to repent,
Just one last example to leave little doubt—
Here's how it feels:

Joel Lipman Poet Laureate of Lucas County, Ohio

inflammatory conditions

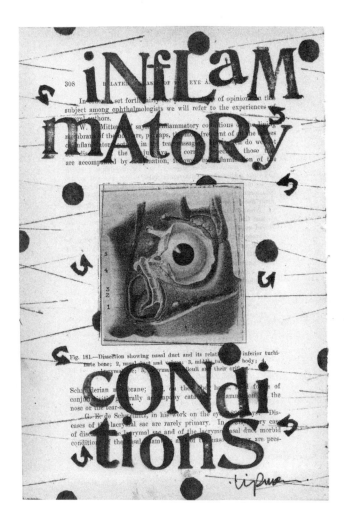

WHAT CAN YOU DO?

"Pick up the phone. Call friends and colleagues. Host a neighborhood or community meeting. Speak up in church. Suggest some action. Sign a petition. Attend a vigil. Lead a prayer. Report acts of hate-fueled vandalism, as a neighborhood or a community. Use whatever skills and means you have. Offer your print shop to make fliers. Share your musical talents at a rally. Give your employees the afternoon off to attend. Be creative. Take action. Do your part to fight hate."

With a very special thanks to the Southern Poverty Law Center, which graciously contributed the chapter headings from its community guide, *Ten Ways to Fight Hate*. Please visit https://www. splcenter.org for more information.

That passionate syllabus
The graybeards all condemn:
Love splendidly impious
Laughing at them! ...
Superbly impious
We laugh at them!

—ending to "The Bright Blasphemy," by Joseph
Auslander, United States Poet Laureate 1937–1941,
born in Philadelphia, published in *The Lyric West*,
April 1922

"If only we could make peace"

—from "If Only" by Sarah Sadie (Busse), Poet
Laureate of Madison, Wisconsin, 2012–2015

Contributors

Martin Achatz lives in Ishpeming, Michigan. He has taught at Western Michigan University and is a contingent professor of English at Northern Michigan University, where he served as Poetry Editor of *Passages North*. His work has appeared in *Kennesaw Review*, *Paterson Literary Review*, and others, as well as in his collection *The Mysteries of the Rosary* (2004). His favorite social justice organization is Room at the Inn, an organization that provides shelter and food for the homeless of the Upper Peninsula.

James Armstrong is the author of two poetry books, *Monument in a Summer Hat* (1999) and *Blue Lash* (2006), and is co-author of *Nature, Culture, and Two Friends Talking* (2015). Originally from Kalamazoo, he lives in Winona, Minnesota, where he was Poet Laureate from 2007 to 2009. He is an active member of the Land Stewardship Project, which stands up for sustainable farming practices and sustainable communities against the corporatization of agriculture.

Columbia University graduate and faculty member **Joseph Auslander** published multiple books, including *Sunrise Trumpets* (1924), *Cyclops' Eye* (1926), *The Winged Horse Anthology* (1929), *No Traveler Returns* (1933), and *More Than Bread* (1936). His collection *The Unconquerables* (1943) addressed Europe's German-occupied countries. From 1937 to 1941, he served as the first Consultant in Poetry to the Library of Congress. Auslander was born in Philadelphia, Pennsylvania, in 1897.

Aliki Barnstone is a poet, translator, critic, editor, and visual artist whose publications include eight books of poetry, including *Dwelling* (2016) and *The*

Collected Poems of C. P. Cavafy (2006). She grew up in Indiana, is Professor of English at the University of Missouri, and serves as Poet Laureate of Missouri.

Siduri Beckman is a lifelong Philadelphian. She focuses her advocacy primarily around equal access to education and criminal justice reform. She is pursuing a B.A. in history with a concentration in human rights at Yale College. In high school, Beckman served as Philadelphia's inaugural Youth Poet Laureate under Poet Laureate and mentor Sonia Sanchez. Her favorite social justice organization is the Southern Poverty Law Center.

Marvin Bell, born in the Bronx and educated at Alfred University and the University of Chicago, taught forty years for the Iowa Writers' Workshop, led a summer program for teachers from the urban program America SCORES, and published the first books of fifteen poets in the series *New Poets/Short Books* (2007–2011). He served as Iowa's first Poet Laureate. His recent book is *Vertigo* (2011). His favorite social justice organization is the Washington Low Income Housing Alliance, and, more specifically, the Compass Housing Alliance, which runs Peter's Place, named for J. Peter Shapiro.

Gail Bellamy, PhD—Cleveland Heights, Ohio, Poet Laureate, April 2009–April 2011 and Cuyahoga Arts and Culture 2010 Creative Workforce Fellowship recipient in poetry—is an award-winning journalist and longtime member of the Society of Professional Journalists. Her seven published books include two poetry chapbooks. She was board president of the Poets & Writers League of Greater Cleveland/Literary Center, 2000–2006. She supports the Society of Professional Journalists' First Amendment Forever Fund, a permanent endowment for press advocacy. SPJ members believe that public enlightenment is the forerunner of justice and the foundation of democracy.

Kimberly Blaeser, professor of creative writing and Native American literature at the University of Wisconsin–Milwaukee and MFA faculty member for Institute of American Indian Arts in Santa Fe, served as Wisconsin Poet Laureate for 2015–2016. The author of three poetry collections including

Apprenticed to Justice (2007) and *Absentee Indians & Other Poems* (2002), Blaeser is Anishinaabe, enrolled at White Earth. She recommends the organization Honor the Earth.

From 1945 to 1946 **Louise Bogan** was the fourth U.S. Poet Laureate appointed to the Library of Congress. Known as part of the "reactionary generation," her poems have been called "masterpieces." Her books include *Body of This Death* (1923), *Dark Summer* (1929), *Sleeping Fury* (1937), *Achievement in American Poetry, 1900–1950* (1951), *Collected Poems, 1923–1953* (1954), and *The Blue Estuaries: Poems, 1923–1968* (1968). Bogan died in 1970 in New York City.

Carson Borbely is a writer of fiction and poetry. She was the 2016 Ann Arbor Youth Poet Laureate and represented Ann Arbor at Brave New Voices International Youth Poetry Slam in 2014 and 2015. She studies global health, writing, and design at Washington University in St. Louis, Missouri.

George Bowering, then living in Port Colborne, Ontario, was Canada's first Parliamentary Poet Laureate, 2002 until 2004. Half a century before, he lied about his age to join a fruit packers union in the Okanagan Valley. His poetry books include *My Darling Nellie Grey* (2010) and *The World, I Guess* (2015). He is an officer of the Order of Canada. The Society for the Prevention of Cruelty to Animals (SPCA) is often listed as a charity; he would like to see it considered an important social organization.

Christopher Bursk, author of thirteen books, most recently *A Car Stops and A Door Opens* (2017), worked in the criminal justice system for three decades. Most importantly he is the grandfather of six. His favorite social justice organization is the Peace Center.

Sarah Sadie (Busse)'s most recent book is *We are traveling through dark at tremendous speeds* (2016). From 2012 to 2015 she shared the Madison Poet Laureate position with her colleague and collaborator, Wendy Vardaman. A lifetime Midwesterner, she has visited every Great Lake and admits a preference for Superior. She is the founder of Odonata Creative. She's inspired by, and grateful to, the Overpass Light Brigade, which exists at the intersection of activism and art, for shining their light since 2011's Wisconsin Uprising.

Carla Christopher is the award-winning and multiply published fourth Poet Laureate of York, Pennsylvania. She is a cultural educator and diversity trainer specializing in African American and LGBTQA issues, and a dynamic international public speaker. She is also a professional community organizer and a seminarian at United Lutheran Seminary at Gettysburg. She recommends Lutheran Advocacy Pennsylvania.

Patricia Clark is Poet-in-Residence and Professor in the Department of Writing at Grand Valley State University, and author of five volumes of poetry. She was Poet Laureate of Grand Rapids, MI from 2005–2007. Clark's latest book is *The Canopy* (2016). She has also published the chapbooks *Given the Trees* (2009) and *Wreath for the Red Admiral* (2016). A new chapbook, *Deadlifts* (2018), was just published. She recommends PEN America.

The fourth Poet Laureate of Toronto (2012–2015) and seventh Parliamentary Poet Laureate (1/1/2016–12/31/2017), **George Elliott Clarke** holds eight honorary doctorates and one PhD. His recognitions include the Governor General's Award for poetry, the National Magazine Award for poetry, an Eric Hoffer Book Award for poetry, and the Premiul Poesis (Romania). He likes the Black Panther Party for Self-Defense.

284

Deborah Cooper is the author of six volumes of poetry, most recently *Blue Window* (2017). She co-edited the anthology *Amethyst and Agate* (2015). She lives in Duluth, Minnesota, close to Lake Superior's North Shore, and summers in Cornucopia, Wisconsin, on the lake's South Shore. She was 2012–2014 Poet Laureate of Duluth. Cooper has conducted writing circles with homeless individuals in her community and taught poetry classes at the county jail for ten years; a community organization that is close to her heart is the Life House, a shelter and resource center for homeless teens.

Tom Cull, Poet Laureate for the City of London, Ontario (2016–2018), teaches creative writing at Western University and runs Thames River Rally, an environmental group he co-founded with his partner Miriam Love. Thames River Rally works to protect river habitat, enhance water quality, and foster citizen stewardship. Cull's chapbook is *What the Badger Said* (2013). His recommended social justice organization is Canadian Freshwater Alliance/ Alliance d'eau douce du Canada.

Craig Czury, 2010–2012 Poet Laureate of Berks County Pennsylvania, spent decades conducting energetic poetry, life-writing, and writing-as-healing workshops in schools, prisons, universities, community centers, juvenile detention centers, homeless shelters, and mental hospitals. Author of over twenty books of poetry, most recently *Fifteen Stones* (2017) and *Thumb Notes Almanac* (2016), Czury lives in Italy, where he teaches poetry writing in a school for the sciences. His favorite social justice organization is the Catholic Worker Movement.

Emilio DeGrazia, born and raised in Dearborn, Michigan, attended Albion College and Ohio State. Now living in Winona, Minnesota, he founded *Great River Review* in 1977 and has won awards for his fiction. He has been a social activist for several decades. *Seasonings* (2012) is his first collection of poetry. He served two terms as Winona's Poet Laureate (2012–2016). His recommended organization is Médicins Sans Frontières (MSF)/Doctors Without Borders.

Rita Dove, a native of Akron, Ohio, served as U.S. Poet Laureate (1993–1995) and Poet Laureate of Virginia (2004–2006). Her many honors include the 1987 Pulitzer Prize for Poetry, the 1996 National Humanities Medal, and the 2011 National Medal of Arts. Her most recent book is *Collected Poems 1974–2004* (2016). She teaches at the University of Virginia. She is a passionate supporter of the Southern Poverty Law Center.

As a Clevelander on Lake Erie, **Cavana I. O. Faithwalker** started Metabedu Connects, facilitating social justice best practices. Faithwalker received a Community Engagement Award (1997) and an Excellence in Programming and Inclusion Award (2000), centered on poetry, jazz, art, and coffeehouse culture. Faithwalker has published in *Art Crimes 21* (2006) and *Trumpet Call* (2012). He was Poet Laureate, City of Cleveland Heights, Ohio, 2011–2013.

Faithwalker recommends the Center for Community Change, Washington, DC, as a great social justice venue.

Sandra Fees is Berks County Poet Laureate, 2016–2018. She is the author of two poetry chapbooks: *The Temporary Vase of Hands* (2017) and *Moving and Being Moved* (2017). She is a Unitarian Universalist minister and resides in Reading, Pennsylvania. She recommends the Unitarian Universalist Service Committee, focused on human rights through grassroots collaboration.

Jim Ferris is Poet Laureate of Lucas County, Ohio, 2015–2019. His books include *The Hospital Poems* (2004) and *Slouching Towards Guantanamo* (2011). President of the Disabled & D/deaf Writers Caucus (2016–2018) and past President of the Society for Disability Studies, Ferris holds the Ability Center Endowed Chair in Disability Studies at the University of Toledo. His recommended social justice organization is ADAPT.

Patricia J. Goodrich is both a poet and a visual artist. Featured at writers' conferences in Romania, Russia, Slovenia, Lithuania, and the United States, she has received Pennsylvania Fellowships in Poetry and Creative Nonfiction. Her poetry collections include *Red Mud* (2009), *Verda's House* (2010), *How the Moose Got To Be* (2012), *Woman with a Wandering Eye* (2014), and *Stone Hunting in Transylvania*, English and Romanian editions (2018). Her social justice organization is A Woman's Place of Bucks County, Pennsylvania.

286

Donald Hall was born in 1928. After graduating from college, Hall spent six years on writing fellowships. When he needed to look for a job, it was time to move outside the East Coast and he taught at the University of Michigan for seventeen years. From 2006 to 2007 he was United States Poet Laureate. For progressive action, he especially admires the American Civil Liberties Union.

Pauletta Hansel is the author of six poetry collections, including *Tangle* (2015) and *Palindrome* (2017), and winner of the 2017 Weatherford Award for Best Appalachian Poetry. She is co-editor of *Pine Mountain Sand & Gravel*, the literary publication of Southern Appalachian Writers Cooperative, and a core member of the Urban Appalachian Community Coalition. She is Cincinnati's first Poet Laureate (2016–2018). Social justice organization recommendation: Greater Cincinnati Homeless Coalition. In addition to its advocacy and education work, it is the publisher of *Streetvibes*, an alternative newspaper that includes creative writing, poetry, articles, photography, and interviews written by homeless and formerly homeless individuals.

Rob Hardy is the first Poet Laureate of Northfield, Minnesota (2016–2019), and a member of the Northfield School Board. He is the author of *Domestication: Collected Poems 1996–2016* (2017) and a recipient of the Making a Difference Award from the Northfield Healthy Community Initiative for his youth advocacy. His recommended social justice organization is TruArtSpeaks in Minneapolis, for which the mission is to cultivate literacy, leadership, and social justice through spoken word and hip-hop culture. Among the programs it sponsors are the annual Be Heard Youth Poetry Slam Series and the Saint Paul Youth Poet Laureate.

The author of poetry, fiction, essays, and plays, **Samuel Hazo** is the International Poetry Forum founder and director in Pittsburgh, Pennsylvania. He's also McAnulty Distinguished Professor of English Emeritus at Duquesne University, where he taught for forty-three years. Hazo was a National Book Award finalist (1973). Governor Robert Casey named him Pennsylvania's first State Poet in 1993, serving until 2003.

David Helwig was born in Toronto, spent years living by the Niagara River and later moved to Kingston, on the St Lawrence. He won the Atlantic Poetry Prize (now the J. M. Abraham Poetry Award) for *The Year One* (2004). From 2008 to 2009 he was Prince Edward Island Poet Laureate. During the 1960s he led discussion groups for inmates in the penitentiary Collins Bay Institution. Médicins Sans Frontières (MSF)/Doctors Without Borders is the social justice organization that he supports with his donations.

Dennis Hinrichsen has authored seven books of poetry, most recently *Skin Music* (2015), co-winner of the 2014 Michael Waters Poetry Prize from

Southern Indiana Review Press. Previous books have won the Akron Poetry Prize (1999), FIELD Poetry Prize (2008), and *Tampa Review* Poetry Prize (2010). He lives in Lansing, Michigan, where he serves as the area's first Poet Laureate. He supports Causa Justa/Just Cause in Oakland, California.

Meredith Holmes lives in Cleveland Heights, Ohio, and in 2005 was the city's first Poet Laureate. She served a second term in 2015. She has two collections of her poems: *Shubad's Crown* (2003) and *Familiar at First Then Strange* (2015). She is a freelance writer, specializing in environmental issues and women in science, engineering, and politics. She supports the anti-gun-violence group Everytown for Gun Safety.

Zora Howard is a Harlem-bred multidisciplinary creator and performer. In 2010 she was named the inaugural New York City Youth Poet Laureate by the Office of the Mayor and released her first collection of poems, *Clutch* (2010). Her work has been showcased on HBO, TV One, PBS, and NBC. She holds a BA from Yale University and an MFA from UCSD. She recommends The Brotherhood/Sister Sol.

Christine Howey, Poet Laureate of Cleveland Heights, Ohio (2016–2018), was the recipient of the Torch Award for leadership by the Cleveland chapter of the Human Rights Campaign. She is a playwright, performance poet, actor, director, and theater critic for *Cleveland Scene*. Her one-person play about her transgender journey, *Exact Change,* was turned into a feature film in 2017. Her recommended social justice organization is Human Rights Campaign.

Karla Huston, Wisconsin Poet Laureate 2017–2018, lives in Appleton, Wisconsin. Her books include *A Theory of Lipstick* (2013) and eight chapbooks of poetry, most recently *Grief Bone* (2017). Huston won a Pushcart Prize for "Theory of Lipstick" and appeared in the *Pushcart Prize XXXVI: Best of the Small Presses* (2012). Her recommended organization is the American Association of Retired Persons (AARP) Public Policy Institute.

Larry Jensen, born and raised in the small Great Lakes city of Owen Sound,

Ontario, is the writer, engineer, and producer of over fifteen CDs, most recently with fellow Poet Laureate 2015–2017 Rob Rolfe, *Mudtown Songs and Poetry* (2016). In 2009 Larry was awarded the very first Owen Sound Cultural Award. He has written songs for Habitat for Humanity. He recommends the Blue Communities Project, which calls on communities to adapt a water commons framework by recognizing water and sanitation as human rights; banning or phasing out the sale of bottled water in municipal facilities and at municipal events; and promoting publicly financed, owned, and operated water and waste services.

David Jones is a Philadelphia native, poet, writer, performer, Temple University student, and Youth Poet Laureate Emeritus (2015–2016) of Philadelphia. Jones found his love for words at a young age, but he didn't find himself on a stage until he was twelve. It started with self-expression, but now it is about healing.

Otter Jung-Allen is a genderqueer poet and performer raised in West Philly. Their work most often centers on celebration for its own sake and the inevitable emotion of growth. They are a 2015 Brave New Voices World Champion, the 2015 Liberty Unplugged Champion, and the 2016–2017 Youth Poet Laureate of Philadelphia. Jung-Allen's work has been published by the American Library of Poetry, *Title Magazine*, and Michigan State University Press.

George Kalamaras, former Poet Laureate of Indiana (2014–2016), is the author of fifteen books of poetry, eight of which are full-length, including *Kingdom of Throat-Stuck Luck* (2011), winner of the Elixir Press 11th Annual Poetry Award. He is Professor of English at Purdue University Fort Wayne, where he has taught since 1990. He recommends HoundSong Rescue.

Rick Kearns is a poet, writer, teacher, and musician of Boricua (Puerto Rican) and European heritage from Harrisburg, Pennsylvania. He was named Poet Laureate of Harrisburg in January 2014. His poems have appeared in over seventy journals, including *The Massachusetts Review, Painted Bride Quarterly*, and *Chicago Review*. Kearns's poems are also in two books, five national anthologies, and seven chapbooks.

L. S. Klatt's poems have appeared widely in magazines and anthologies, including *The Best American Poetry*, *Poetry Daily*, *Harvard Review*, *The Believer*, *Blackbird*, and *The Common*. His latest volume is a collection of prose poems entitled *The Wilderness After Which* (2017). He recently completed a three-year term as Poet Laureate of Grand Rapids, Michigan. His favorite social justice organization is the Association for a More Just Society.

Karen Kovacik, former Indiana Poet Laureate, is professor of English at Indiana University–Purdue University Indianapolis. She is the author of two poetry collections, *Beyond the Velvet Curtain* (1999) and *Metropolis Burning* (2005), and the editor of *Scattering the Dark: An Anthology of Polish Women Poets* (2016). Her poems and translations of contemporary Polish poetry have appeared widely. Her favorite social justice organization is Indiana Undocumented Youth Alliance (IUYA).

Norbert Krapf, former Indiana Poet Laureate, has published eleven collections, including *Bloodroot* (2008) and *Catholic Boy Blues* (2015). Some of his subjects: the Holocaust, the treatment of the Miami Indians, the life of Ida Hagan from the Pinkston Freedom Settlement, and surviving child abuse by a priest. He has collaborated with jazz pianist Monika Herzig and bluesman Gordon Bonham. His favorite social justice organization is Peace Learning Center in Indianapolis.

Thomas Leduc lives in the City of Greater Sudbury, Ontario, and often visits Manitoulin Island in Lake Huron. He was Poet Laureate of the City of Greater Sudbury 2014–2016 and is president of the Sudbury Writers' Guild. He has been published in numerous anthologies and magazines, including Laurentian University's Literary Journal *Sulphur*. His social justice organization is Girls Inc.; one of its commercials partly inspired the poem included in this anthology.

John B. Lee was appointed Poet Laureate of the City of Brantford in perpetuity in 2004 and Poet Laureate of Norfolk County for life in 2014. He lives in a lake house overlooking Long Point Bay on Lake Erie. In 2017 he received the

Canada 150 Medal "for his outstanding contribution to literary development both at home and abroad." He recommends the Alzheimer Society of Canada/ Société Alzheimer Canada.

M. L. Liebler is an internationally known Detroit poet, professor, literary arts activist, and arts organizer. The author of fifteen books and chapbooks, Liebler has taught at Wayne State University since 1980. He has been the Poet Laureate of St. Clair Shores, Michigan, since 2005. He edited the groundbreaking anthology *Working Words* (2010). In 2017 Liebler published three award-winning books. He has been involved with The Catholic Worker Movement since 1990.

Appointed the first Poet Laureate of Lucas County (2008–2014) by the Board of County Commissioners, **Joel Lipman** was raised in Kenosha, Wisconsin, and has lived in Chicago, Buffalo, and Toledo. He is a recipient of Ohio's Governor's Award and five Ohio Arts Council fellowships. His poems appear in *Inland Seas* of the National Museum of the Great Lakes. His recommended social justice organization is Advocates for a Clean Lake Erie, an "environmental organization founded in Toledo, Ohio, to protect the Western Lake Erie Basin and the communities that depend on it."

damian lopes, Poet Laureate, City of Barrie, 2014–2018, was born in Scotland but raised on a tributary to Lake Ontario. lopes lives on Lake Simcoe and cottages upstream of Georgian Bay. A writer/member of PEN Canada and The Writers' Union of Canada, his poetry includes *sensory deprivation* (2000), *clay lamps & fighter kites* (2000), and *yasser arafat is dead* (2015). His recommended social justice organization is PEN Canada.

Sue MacLeod was Poet Laureate of Halifax Regional Municipality from 2001 to 2005. She has also lived in Toronto, where she liked strolling on the boardwalk beside Lake Ontario. Her most recent books are a young adult novel, *Namesake* (2013), and a poetry collection, *Mood Swing, with Pear* (2016). She now lives in Montréal and recommends that city's Old Brewery Mission, which supports the homeless and works to end homelessness.

Naomi Long Madgett, Poet Laureate of Detroit since 2001, is the author of ten books of poetry and two textbooks, and has edited two anthologies. Her poems appear in more than one hundred and eighty anthologies in the United States and abroad. She is a Professor of English Emerita at Eastern Michigan University and was publisher and editor of Lotus Press for forty-three years. She has been awarded an American Book Award (1993), four honorary degrees, and several lifetime achievement awards.

Laren McClung is the author of a collection of poems, *Between Here and Monkey Mountain* (2012), and editor for the anthology *Inheriting the War: Poetry and Prose by Descendants of Vietnam Veterans and Refugees* (2017). She teaches at New York University and lives in Bucks County where she was the 2016 Poet Laureate. She supports Kundiman, a nonprofit dedicated to nurturing generations of writers and readers of Asian American literature, as well as the William Joiner Institute for the Study of War and Social Consequences.

Ken McCullough is in his third term as Poet Laureate of Winona, Minnesota. He lived in the Upper Peninsula for some of his teenage years and is a recent convert to Lake Superior. His most recent books of poetry are *Broken Gates* (2012) and *Dark Stars* (2017). He continues to be involved in causes related to Native America; one organization he recommends is the Cheyenne River Indian Outreach.

Peter Meinke received his MA in English literature from the University of Michigan (1961). His latest collection is *Lucky Bones* (2014, his eighth in the Pitt Poetry Series). His collection *The Piano Tuner* received the 1986 Flannery O'Connor Award for Short Fiction. His work has appeared in *Poetry, The New Yorker,* and other magazines. He's currently Poet Laureate of Florida (2015–2019). He and his wife, the artist Jeanne Clark Meinke, are very supportive of Planned Parenthood in difficult times; a second Planned Parenthood Health Center has just opened in St. Pete.

Oscar Mireles, the sixth—and first Latino—Poet Laureate of the City of Madison, Wisconsin (2016–2020), has been the Executive Director of Omega

School, an adult learning center, for the past twenty-three years, assisting over five thousand GED/HSED graduates. Mireles served as publisher/editor of three anthologies titled *I Didn't Know There Were Latinos in Wisconsin* (1989, 1999, 2014). He recommends Voces de la Frontera Milwaukee.

Roger Nash is inaugural Poet Laureate of the City of Greater Sudbury (2009–2011) and past president of the League of Canadian Poets. His awards include the Canadian Jewish Book Award for Poetry (1997) and the PEN/O. Henry Prize Story Award (2009). His most recent poetry collection is *Whazzat?* (2017). He promotes lake conservation with the Vale Living with Lakes Centre (Laurentian University). He recommends and organizes for Women's Legal Education and Action Fund (LEAF), which fights for precedent-setting charter rights cases for women in Canadian courts and promotes public education and social change.

Thomas O'Connell, 2015–2016 Beacon, New York, Poet Laureate, is a librarian living on the banks of the Hudson River. His poetry and short fiction have appeared in *Jellyfish Review*, *Elm Leaves Journal*, *The Los Angeles Review*, and *Hobart*, as well as other print and online journals.

Howard D. Paap resides in Bayfield, Wisconsin, where he was named the town's Poet Laureate for 2017–2018. He taught anthropology for over thirty years on Minnesota and Wisconsin college campuses. His several publications include *Red Cliff, Wisconsin* (2013). A veteran of the U.S. Navy, he now writes for the *Ashland Daily Press*. He recommends the American Civil Liberties Union of Wisconsin; this organization recently stepped up regarding the recent shooting of an Ojibwe teen at Bad River by a white Ashland Police officer.

Sheila Packa was Duluth Poet Laureate 2010–2012. She has four books, *The Mother Tongue* (2007), *Echo & Lightning* (2010), *Cloud Birds* (2011), and *Night Train Red Dust* (2014), and recently collaborated with Helsinki composer Olli Kortekangas. The Minnesota Orchestra premiered their work *Migrations* in 2016. She teaches at Lake Superior College and in the community. She supports the American Civil Liberties Union.

Tony Pena has been selected as the 2017–2018 Poet Laureate for the City of Beacon, New York. He is the author of a collection of poetry and flash fiction, *Blood and Beats and Rock 'n' Roll* (2016), and has created videos of his poetry and punk rock-and-roll performances.

Founder of the Upper Peninsula Poet Laureate position (2013–current), **Ron Riekki** has lived in eight Illinois and Michigan cities. He wrote *U.P.* (2008), edited *The Way North* (2013, Michigan Notable Book), *Here* (2015, Independent Publisher Book Award), and *And Here* (2017), and published in *The Threepenny Review*, *Bellevue Literary Review*, *Spillway*, and *Rattle*. He recommends the Brady Center to Prevent Gun Violence.

Rob Rolfe is the author of five books of poetry: *The Hawk* (2008), *Saugeen* (2011), *Beyond Mudtown* (2013), *Hard Times* (2015), and *Hart Rouge* (2017). He served as Owen Sound Poet Laureate for 2015–2017 with singer-songwriter Larry Jensen. He was active in Canada's largest union, the Canadian Union of Public Employees (CUPE), in its efforts to combat racism and discrimination. His recommended social justice organization is Hamilton Coalition to Stop the War, an affiliate of the Canadian Peace Alliance/L'Alliance canadienne pour la paix.

Laurence Sansone is a writer and musician living in Beacon, New York. He held the position of Beacon Poet Laureate from January 1, 2013, to January 1, 2015. In addition to his published writings, he is featured as lead vocalist, songwriter, and lyricist on the 2006 Mapleshade Records release Yucca Flats, *Garden of Weeds*. His favorite social justice organization is Planned Parenthood.

Andrea Scarpino is the author of the collections *Once Upon Wing Lake* (2017), *What the Willow Said as it Fell* (2016), and *Once, Then* (2014). She received a PhD in creative writing from Bath Spa University, has published in numerous journals, and is co-editor of *Nine Mile Magazine*. She served as Poet Laureate of Michigan's Upper Peninsula, 2015–2017. She has many favorite social justice organizations, including the Southern Poverty Law Center, Black Lives Matter, Planned Parenthood, and Forward Through Ferguson.

Ellie Schoenfeld is the 2016–2018 Duluth Poet Laureate. She grew up with Lake Superior always in sight. *The Dark Honey* (2009) was awarded a Northeastern Minnesota Book Award. She is grateful for support from the Arrowhead Regional Arts Council. Schoenfeld has worked with groups to support water quality, treaty rights, women's rights, and antiwar efforts. She recommends Loaves and Fishes Catholic Worker Community in Duluth.

Lisa Russ Spaar is the author and editor of more than ten books, most recently *Monticello in Mind* (2016) and *Orexia* (2017). Her awards include a Guggenheim Fellowship and she has been shortlisted for a National Book Critics Circle Award for Excellence in Reviewing. Her mother was born and raised in Detroit; her parents met at the University of Michigan and made sure their children knew the beauty of the Great Lakes.

Kevin Stein has published eleven books of poetry, scholarship, and anthology, including *American Ghost Roses* (2005), winner of a Society of Midland Authors Award, and the essay collection *Poetry's Afterlife* (2011). He served as Illinois Poet Laureate from 2003 to 2017.

Barbara Buckman Strasko is the first Poet Laureate of Lancaster County, Pennsylvania. She is the 2009 River of Words Teacher of the Year. Her poems have appeared in *Best New Poets*, *Ninth Letter* and *Poet Lore*. Her book of poems is *Graffiti in Braille* (2012). Her poem "Bricks and Mortar" is engraved in granite in Lancaster's main square. Her favorite social justice organization is Lancaster Stands Up.

Joyce Sutphen's first collection of poems, *Straight Out of View* (1995), won the Barnard Women Poets Prize, and a recent collection, *Modern Love & Other Myths* (2015), was a finalist for a Minnesota Book Award. She has been the Minnesota Poet Laureate since 2011 and always spends a week or so on Lake Superior. She commends the social justice theatre troupe I Am We Are at Gustavus Adolphus College.

Wisconsin Poet Laureate (2004–2008) **Denise Sweet** is White Earth Anishi-naabe (Bear Clan) and has presented readings in the United States, Mexico, Central America, Europe, and Canada. She has appeared in film and theatre and served as director of the Wisconsin Indian Arts Festival and co-director of the Performing Arts Festival, sponsored by the Diné Nation. Her submission for an organization related to social justice is Indigenous Environmental Network, a tribal-based initiative developing policies and practices for the protection of indigenous-based environments.

Heather H. Thomas is the award-winning author of seven poetry collections, including *Vortex Street* (2018). Her poems are translated into seven languages, including Arabic. She teaches at Cedar Crest College and lives in Reading, Pennsylvania. She was Berks Poet Laureate (Pennsylvania). She recommends Our Children's Trust: Securing the Legal Right to a Safe Climate.

Russell Thorburn is the author of *Somewhere We'll Leave the World* (2017) and first Poet Laureate of the Upper Peninsula. He lives in Marquette, Michigan.

The Poet Laureate of Grand Rapids, Michigan, from 2007 to 2010, **Rodney Torreson** is the author of four books, including two chapbooks. His full-length books are *The Ripening of Pinstripes* (1998) and *A Breathable Light* (2002). His poems have appeared in multiple publications. His favorite social justice organization is Right to Life.

Born in Chicago, **William Trowbridge** published his seventh poetry collection, *Vanishing Point*, in 2017. He also published the graphic chapbook *Oldguy: Superhero* (2016). He is a faculty mentor in the University of Nebraska Omaha Low-Residency MFA in Writing Program and was Poet Laureate of Missouri from 2012 to 2016. His favorite social justice organization is All Souls Unitarian Universalist Church in Kansas City.

A Bronx native, **Crystal Valentine** is a poet, activist, and educator. She is a 2017 Callaloo Fellow, 2015 New York City Youth Poet Laureate, and author of *Not Everything is a Eulogy* (2015). Valentine's work has been featured on programming for MSNBC, Blavity, Button Poetry, The Huffington Post, BET, CNN, *The New York Daily News*, and more. She earned her BA in Psychology at New York University, where she is returning as a Goldwater Fellow and MFA candidate in Poetry.

Wendy Vardaman is the author of three poetry collections and lives in Madison, Wisconsin (Poet Laureate 2012–2015). She has worked as a writing teacher; an arts administrator at a children's theater; a freelance editor-writer-teacher-designer; and an assistant editor and Web manager in the architectural glass industry. She recently returned to school to study graphic and Web design, letterpress, and printmaking. For social justice organizations, she recommends Woodland Pattern Book Center in Milwaukee.

Shari Wagner, Indiana's fifth Poet Laureate (2016–2017), is the author of two books of poetry: *The Harmonist at Nightfall: Poems of Indiana* (2013), and *Evening Chore* (2005). She has an MFA in creative writing from Indiana University and teaches for the Indiana Writers Center in Indianapolis. Her favorite social justice organization is the service agency of the Mennonite Church, MCC (Mennonite Central Committee).

A native of the Kootenays, **Fred Wah** lives in Vancouver. He earned an MA from SUNY Buffalo. Canada's fifth Parliamentary Poet Laureate, he's an officer of the Order of Canada. Wah has published and edited poetry, fiction, and criticism since the 1960s. Recent collections: *Sentenced to Light* (2008), *is a door* (2009), and *Scree: The Collected Earlier Poems, 1962–1991* (2016).

Mary Weems is a poet, playwright, foundations scholar, and former Poet Laureate of Cleveland Heights (2007–2009). Weems's thirteen books include *Blackeyed* (2014), *Writings of Healing and Resistance* (2012), *For(e)closure* (2012), and *An Unmistakable Shade of Red and the Obama Chronicles* (2008). She is a recipient of the Cleveland Arts Prize Emerging Artist Award. She recommends the Social Justice Institute at Case Western Reserve University, founded by Rhonda Williams and Theatre Artists for Social Change (TASC), a collaboration between Dobama Theatre and Karamu Performing Arts Center.

Yolanda Wisher is the author of *Monk Eats an Afro* (2014) and co-editor of *Peace is a Haiku Song* (2013). Wisher performs a unique blend of poetry and song with her band The Afroeaters. A Pew Fellow and Hedgebrook Writer-in-Residence, Wisher was named the inaugural Poet Laureate of Montgomery County, Pennsylvania, in 1999 and the third Poet Laureate of Philadelphia in 2016. Her favorite social justice organization is Contemporary Black Canvas.

Anna Yin was Mississauga's first Poet Laureate (2015–2016). Her books include *Wings Towards Sunlight* (2011) and *Seven Nights with the Chinese Zodiac* (2015). Yin received two MARTY Awards and 2016/2017 WCU Poetry Conference scholarships. Her poems have appeared in *Arc Poetry*, *The New York Times*, *China Daily*, CBC Radio, *World Journal*, *Literary Review of Canada*, and more. She recommends World Vision International.

Liz Zetlin lives on the Sydenham River, near Georgian Bay. She was Owen Sound's inaugural Poet Laureate (2007–2009); Owen Sound's Outstanding Individual in the Arts (2013); and co-founder and artistic director of the Words Aloud Spoken Word Festival. Her latest poetry book is *The Punctuation Field* (2011). As chair of the Owen Sound Water Watchers, she works closely with the Council of Canadians, which she highly recommends.

Inaugural City of Mississauga Youth Poet Laureate **Rebecca Zseder** is a student at the University of Toronto Mississauga. She is an English specialist and hopes to publish her first poetry compilation before her graduation in 2020. Her passion for writing stems from her passion for people. She plans to forever continue making literature out of life.